STOP THE WORLD I WANT TO GET ON

C. PETER WAGNER

A Division of G/L Publications
Glendale, California, U.S.A.

...ing
...
Latin American Theology (Wm. B. Eerdmans
  Publishing Co.)
The Protestant Movement in Bolivia (William
  Carey Library)
An Extension Seminary Primer (with Ralph
  Covell; William Carey Library)
A Turned-on Church in an Uptight World
  (Zondervan Publishing House)
Frontiers in Missionary Strategy (Moody Press)
Church/Mission Tensions Today (editor, Moody
  Press)
Look Out! The Pentecostals Are Coming
  (Creation House)

© Copyright 1974 by C. Peter Wagner
All rights reserved

Second Printing, 1975

Published by Regal Books Division, G/L Publications
Glendale, California 91209
Printed in U.S.A.

Library of Congress Catalog Card No. 73-80093
Hardcover edition: ISBN 0-8307-0272-5
Softcover edition: ISBN 0-8307-0271-7

To
Herb and Margo

Contents

Letter to the Reader

You've heard it. Maybe you've even said it. . . .

"Missions aren't for me!

"Look, friend. I'm a Christian all right, but the Christian life involves an awful lot, and you have to be a little choosy. Missions? They're okay for the ladies on Tuesday afternoons; I suppose somebody has to wrap bandages for missionaries. And then, take our Missions Sunday every March. You know—the guy with the baggy suit who gets his kids up on the stage to sing in some foreign language. I sit through it just like everybody else in church, but that's all the missions I need for the year."

Too bad!

It's a shame that so many Christians have formed their opinions of missions on the basis of the women's missionary society or after hearing some returned missionary who still hadn't recovered from his reverse culture shock after five years in Mamba Bamba.

That's as bad as judging all Germans by Hitler. Or saying you don't like to eat in restaurants because Joe's Diner serves lumpy gravy.

I'm writing this book, for one thing, to suggest that if you're still clutching some stereotyped ideas of missions, you're out of it. If you step back and take a look at the whole picture, you will soon be aware that the Christian church—especially in America, but also in other parts of the world—shifted into high gear when it rounded the curve from the 1960s to the 1970s. All signals are *go* right now.

You're right—missions aren't *all* there is to the Christian life. But living the Christian life today without a solid involvement in missions is like touring France without seeing the Eiffel Tower, or going to the beach without getting wet, or kissing your sister. No way!

There is so much action and excitement in missions today that many missionaries themselves have trouble keeping up. More missionaries than ever before are building refresher courses into their furlough periods. Pastors who are with it are expanding their church's missionary conferences because it gives their whole congregation a tremendous pickup. Publishers are begging for more manuscripts on missions, and the books are getting better all the time. In some Christian circles, if you can't discuss ethnotheology, the cultural versus the evangelistic mandate, or what missionaries are saying about apartheid in South Africa, you are considered poorly informed.

One of the great signs of the times is the current attitude of young people toward missions. David Howard, who heads the missionary department of Inter-Varsity Christian Fellowship, recently told me that today's college students are more turned on by missions than he has ever observed before. He said that during the summer of 1972, in the orientation sessions for new IVCF staff, for the first time in several years he no longer had to *defend* foreign missions. The new staff had already absorbed much of the general excitement about missions; they just wanted Howard to tell them what they could do to get themselves and other students more involved in what God is doing in the world.

When something as colorful and as important as the world mission of the Christian Church is zooming along at the rate it is today, you probably want to get on board, too. This book is designed to help you do it. It stops the world of contemporary missions for a minute and says, "Hey, the ride's great. Jump on!"

But, hurry. It won't stop for long. . . .

Pete

C. Peter Wagner

Look What God's Doing

CHAPTER 1

Springtime has come for Christian missions.

The world always has some effect on the church. It did back through the 1960s, when Christian missions were passing through a cold winter. The massive, worldwide retreat of the colonial powers from their empires following World War II, the Viet Nam War, the violent struggles for civil rights in the U.S.A., student revolts, and the formation of counter-cultures—all combined to create an oppressive cloud of pessimism and defeatism for Americans in general and American Christians in particular.

It looked to some as though the thaw would never come. A professor of missions wrote a book entitled *Missionary, Go Home*. The large mainline denominations found missionary giving dropping drastically, and hundreds of missionary couples who returned on furlough were told that they could no longer be supported and that they had to seek a ministry here at home. Disillusioned missionary leaders began talking about a postmissionary era. Some even wondered whether the missionary movement had failed.

1

Even now, although people should know better, a gurgle from the past is heard here and there. As late as 1973, a leading magazine published an article alleging that missionary societies will soon disappear, the sooner the better, and that Christian businessmen ought to develop a program to provide housing for jaded missionaries. Understandably, the author remained anonymous. He was really out of it!

Just the opposite is true. Mission leaders with their fingers on the pulse of what God is doing in the world today agree that we now have begun to move into the springtime of missions. The frost has gone from the ground, the grass is turning green, and daffodils are springing up all over. The sun is warm, the sky is blue. Oh, we have our share of April showers, but they are producing May flowers in abundance.

Predicting the Future

You don't need a crystal ball to predict that during the 1970s the number of missionary societies will increase, not decrease. Some of them might be quite different from the old-fashioned Western model, granted. As a matter of fact, most of the newer ones will probably not be Western at all—they will spring up from Asia, Africa and Latin America, as we will see in detail in chapter 8. The number of missionaries will increase, but qualifications may change. Missionary budgets will swell, but different priorities will exist for spending money. We can be quite certain that every year will see more men and women won to Christ and more Christian churches planted around the world than any previous year.

It is true that Britain no longer rules the waves, but this has not stopped God. As keen a Christian thinker as Bishop Stephen Neill has taken a sweeping look at mankind and observed that never in human history has there ever been what might be classified as a universal religion, until today. We now have one that qualifies, and

2

that religion is Christianity! This doesn't sound like modern missions have been a failure.

Other things have changed, however. The "almighty dollar" has lost its sovereignty in the world. The U.S.A. has fought the first war it couldn't win. Wide cracks have appeared in what used to be considered the solid Communist block. The new nations of Africa and Asia are maturing, losing their self-consciousness, and even controlling the voting in the United Nations. Latin-American nations expropriate American businesses and hear hardly a squeak from Washington.

The dramatic rise of the Third World as a strong and mature force in international politics has taken some by surprise, and not everyone has adjusted yet. Of course, it did not take God by surprise. That is why He is working in new ways in our new world. Christians who are keeping up with what God is doing on the planet as a whole have never been more optimistic.

Fifty-five Thousand Christians a Day?

It is hard to believe, but at the present time, according to our best calculations, a minimum of fifty-five thousand people are becoming Christians every day of the year. How do we arrive at this figure?

First of all, we take into account the world population explosion. World population back in the days of Abraham and Moses may have been 100 million or less. At the time of Christ, it had reached 275 million. When William Carey launched the modern missionary movement around 1800, the world population was about 900 million. It passed 1 billion in 1850, 2 billion in the 1930s, and 3 billion around 1970.

The best statistics we have peg the number of Christians in the world at around one billion, or one-third of the world's population. Top missionary statesmen agree that Christianity is more than holding its own as far as world percentage is concerned. The rate of population growth is two percent per year. Christianity is growing at a higher rate, but to be conservative, let's use the two percent figure. This gives us an increase of 20 million Christians a year, or divided by 365, around fifty-five thousand per day.

By now, of course, you may have raised the logical question: What do you mean by *Christians?* This is a very important question, and it must be answered whenever we deal with mission statistics.

Generally speaking, we use two kinds of statistics in what we call "missiology," which means the science of missions. I have given them descriptive labels so as not to confuse them:

1. *World Christian Handbook* statistics. The *World Christian Handbook* is an important statistical survey of Christianity published at irregular intervals (every three to seven years). It lists as Christians everybody who would answer "Christian" if a census taker asked him to state his religion. The new *World Christian Handbook,* due to be released in 1973, will include Catholics for the first time. These statistics include nominal as well as committed Christians, along with all those in between.

2. *Lamb's Book of Life* statistics. The *Lamb's Book of Life* will not be available for publication until the final judgment day. (See Rev. 20:12; 21:27.) God Himself is keeping these statistics, and unfortunately many who are listed in the *World Christian Handbook* are not in the *Lamb's Book of Life.* Only what we call born-again Christians are in the *Lamb's Book of Life.* To qualify, one must be a true child of God, "born, not of blood, nor of the will of the flesh, nor of the will of man, but of God" (John 1:13). It is not enough to be born in a Christian country or even into a Christian family; one must enter God's family through a personal, individual experience with Him.

Missiologists are aware of both these kinds of statistics, and they use them both, but for different purposes. The most obvious problem is that they have the *World Christian Handbook* in their libraries, but not the *Lamb's Book of Life*. This does not mean, however, that no one has any idea who is in the *Lamb's Book of Life*. Though there are always some clever hypocrites, or some tares among the wheat, most perceptive Christians can tell with a good degree of accuracy who in their own family or in their circle of friends are true Christians. It is a little more difficult, but pastors of churches should know their sheep (John 10:14), and they have a fair idea which of their people are Christians in heart and which are Christians only in name.

But when you go from there to the broad, worldwide ecclesiastical statistics, the problem becomes much more complex. How many of the *World Christian Handbook* Christians are *Lamb's Book of Life* Christians? This is a question that could be debated daily in every corner of Christendom, but God alone knows the answer.

For lack of better facts—more realistic information—we simply use the *World Christian Handbook* statistics and let it go at that, recognizing their limitations.

Now notice. This explanation does not lead us to the conclusion that real, true Christianity is increasing at a rate *slower* than Christianity in general. If an angel were to come down and tell us just what percentage of those in the *World Christian Handbook* is also in the *Lamb's Book of Life,* we would doubtless find that we had located those Christians who are growing, not only through population increase (as nominal Christians do), but also through aggressive evangelism that is bringing new non-Christians into the fold. Born-again Christians are *fewer* than nominal Christians, but they are certainly growing *faster*.

The Challenge

The encouraging figure of at least fifty-five thousand new Christians in the world every day might conceivably have the wrong effect on some people. They might say, "Wow! This is great. The job is getting done much faster than I thought. Now we can rest and go on to something else."

Don't fall into that trap!

In order to get the *blessing*, we look at the wonderful way God is bringing people to Himself and building His church. But in order to catch the *challenge*, we look, not at the Christians, but at the *fourth world*.

This expression *fourth world* is one of the handiest new phrases we have. It's so new you won't even find it in the unabridged dictionary. Since I will be repeating it often in this book, let me pause here to explain it.

Words, like clothes, can wear out or go out of style, so that one has to replace them with something better. We have had quite a few outdated words in missionary work, and we are trying to get rid of them. Several words that once were useful and that had positive meanings are now disreputable. Missionaries used to go to the "heathen" or to the "savages" or to the "pagans" or to the "natives" or to a "backward people." These expressions, and others like them, are now almost as degrading to some ears as *nigger* or *wop* or *kike*. Something new was needed.

For some years now, the term *third world* has been in use. There is still some debate as to its precise meaning, but most people who use it refer to those nations that refuse to align themselves with either the Communist block, headed by Russia, or the capitalist block, headed by the United States, and that have decided to be their own masters on the international scene. This world includes, therefore, most of the nations in Africa, Asia, and Latin America. Most of the third world is yellow, black, brown, and red, and most of its people live south of the thirtieth parallel north.

Fourth world is not used to describe some other form of international political alliance or nonalliance. It shifts

6

the focus to spiritual things. By *fourth world* we mean all those people, no matter where they are found, who have yet to commit themselves to Jesus Christ as Saviour. There are fourth world people in Russia, there are some in Africa, there are some in Chicago, Illinois, and there are some in every other tribe, tongue and nation.

It is much better to talk of sending missionaries to the fourth world than to the "heathen," although in the final analysis you're talking about the same thing.

So much for the definition. Now back to the challenge. According to the same world population statistics we have been using, the human race is increasing by 74 million per year. Of this increase, as we have seen, 20 million are Christians. Thus the fourth world is growing by 54 million annually, and dividing by 365 days, we find that *every day 148,000 people are added to the fourth world.*

When it comes right down to it, the *challenge* is greater than the *blessing:* 148,000 as compared to 55,000. This, pure and simple, is the reason why in the days to come Christians have to become *more* involved in missions—not just sit back as though the job were done.

I am often amused by Christians who are overly nostalgic. They say, "My, the Christian church is in terrible shape. If we could only go back to the first century, we would know what God really can do through a dedicated church." I don't think we're perfect today by any means, but I disagree with that perspective. I honestly think that if Luke himself could have the choice, he would rather live today than in the first century. When we lift up our eyes to what God is doing *world wide* today, that early activity around the eastern Mediterranean seems like a small pilot project compared to what is happening now.

Phenomenal Growth in Latin America

In Latin America, for example, the Protestant church is growing at a rate three times that of the population

7

in general. This is all the more striking when you realize that Latin America, with a growth rate of 2.9, is the fastest growing area of the world. The church, however, is growing at about 10 percent per year.

Back in 1900, only fifty thousand Protestants could be found in Latin America. In the 1930s there were 1 million, in the 1940s there were 2 million, in the 1950s there were 5 million, in the 1960s there were 10 million, and already in the 1970s there are over 20 million. Some are predicting 100 million by the end of the century.

Although many groups are seeing good church growth there, over two-thirds of the Protestants in Latin America are Pentecostals. The upsurge of the Pentecostal movement in Latin America is one of the outstanding demonstrations of God's power in the world today. In a book I have just written called *Look Out! The Pentecostals Are Coming*, I have attempted to get below the surface and discover the amazing reasons why this is happening.

Percentagewise, churches have grown faster in Chile than in any other country in Latin America. One of the reasons for this is that Christians continually take their witness to the fourth world by preaching on the streets. In the evenings or on the weekends, you can't go far around the city of Santiago without running into a group of Pentecostals out on the street, singing and preaching. Sometimes it appears that they don't have much of an audience, but testimony after testimony from Chilean brethren declares that they first heard the gospel on a street corner or in a plaza.

One of my favorite churches is the Jotabeche Church in Santiago. For years I visited the old building, which seated only five thousand. They have recently torn that one down, bought more property, and built a new church building that seats sixteen thousand! They even have rooms for two hundred overnight guests, with an independent water and power supply.

8

Latin America is wider open to the gospel than ever before. The Second Vatican Council, held during the early sixties, has put an end to the bitter persecution of Protestants by Roman Catholics that had characterized Latin America. Since then, literally millions of people who previously were only *World Christian Handbook* Christians now have their names in the *Lamb's Book of Life*. In Ecuador, the Quechua Indians, who over the years were resistant to the gospel, have recently turned receptive, and the Gospel Missionary Union is reaping a great harvest there. A full ten million Quechuas in Ecuador, Peru, and Bolivia, however, are still in the fourth world—part of the challenge.

Brazil is seeing some rather phenomenal church growth. The Brazil for Christ Church has about 250,000 baptized members. Their "mother church" in the city of Sao Paulo seats twenty-five thousand, and is thought to be the world's largest church building. They are multiplying largely because they use the mother-daughter system of planting churches. Every established church is responsible for reproducing—for having as many children as possible. Some mother churches have five, ten, or twenty daughter churches.

One group in Bolivia is using a system called "each-church-one-church-in-one-year." Part of the responsibility of each and every church is to plant a new one every twelve months. These Bolivians decided to adopt this practice when they had 20 churches in 1970. By the end of 1971 they had 50 churches, by the end of 1972 they had 104, and they are trusting God for 208 or more by the end of 1973. These churches are being planted among the Aymara Indians, one of the most receptive of the peoples of Latin America.

Two important movements, now worldwide, began in Latin America during the 1960s: the theological education by extension program and Evangelism in Depth, the father

9

of what is now called "saturation evangelism." We shall discuss both these movements later in more detail. A strong "renewal movement" has taken root in Brazil, Argentina and Costa Rica, and is rapidly spreading through churches in most of the Latin American republics. Many churches which had become lazy and nominal are now getting a new lease on life and moving out. In some countries it has been reported that entire villages have turned to Christ.

Some people thought that Marxism would defeat Christianity in Latin America. Although it is true that Marxism is very strong all over the continent, no such defeat has occurred. In Chile, for example, where the first freely elected Marxist president in the world was in control, the churches were not hindered one bit in the aggressive evangelism that has characterized them through the years. In many cases, it seems as though the social revolution makes people more open than ever before to the claims of Christ.

Massive Influx in Africa

I used to think that Christianity couldn't grow faster than it is growing in Latin America. But when I went to Africa for the first time, I found a church that was booming. David Barrett says, "For one hundred years now, the most massive influx into the churches in history has been taking place on the African continent." In 1900 there were about 10 million Christians in Africa. Today there are over 130 million, and the projection for the end of the century is 395 million. Granted, these are *World Christian Handbook*-type statistics, but even so, Christians can hardly do anything but rejoice at an increase from 7.5 percent professing Christians at the beginning of the century to 48.3 percent at the end of the century. No matter how you slice it, God has been at work in Africa.

One of the most remarkable phenomena in church history has been taking place in Africa during the last hundred years. Called the African Independent Church Movement, it has now spread to at least one-third of the tribes in Africa. At least six thousand of these new Christian groups (some more orthodox or biblical than others) have sprung up and include over eight million persons. Some are small with only a few hundred members, and some go into the hundreds of thousands like the Kimbangu Church of Zaire. They are growing at a rate faster than most people can keep track of.

On a recent visit to Kenya I had the privilege of meeting one of the independent leaders personally. Archbishop Herbert Aloo is one of the top leaders of the Maria Legio Church, but not the top. Over the church's archbishops are eight cardinals and one person called the Pope. Aloo told me how they split from the Catholic church back in 1962 because they felt the priests were not living according to the rules of the Bible. They still consider themselves Catholic, but not Roman Catholic. "Everything we do, we do according to the Bible," he affirmed.

Aloo was converted when he was sick. He read about Baba Simeon, the top leader of the movement, in the local newspaper and sought him out. Baba Simeon prayed for him and he was healed. Aloo and the others even call Baba Simeon "Jesus" because through him they were saved, not only from disease, but from drunkenness, fighting, and a degraded life. They have no apparent theological problem with an overidentification of their leader with the Messiah. None of the clergy receives a salary. Aloo must be one of the few archbishops in the world who earns his living as a laborer at the local airport.

But somehow, all this must be relevant to East Africans. The little group of ten that began in 1962 has now grown to 150,000!

Gathering the Harvest in Asia

The continent of Asia is dominated by China, the world's

most populous nation. During the years that China was completely closed, Christians in general were pessimistic about her fate. But the mood is changing radically now that China is participating more in international affairs. Many missiologists think that one of the greatest harvests for Christianity is ripening in China, but they are quick to add that most likely it will not be reaped by traditional methods. What these new reaping methods will be is one of the hot questions in missions.

Even while China was closed, God was doing tremendous things in Asia. The great revival that swept Indonesia during the late 1960s brought an unusual ingathering. In spite of debates among Christian leaders as to exactly how many Indonesians became Christians and whether or not water was turned to wine, no one can fail to discern the tremendous, positive movement of the hand of God there. In 1910 Indonesia had less than one-half million Christians, but today there are something over six million. Recently, for the first time in the history of modern missions, a significant number of Muslims have become Christians.

In spite of the fact that Burma has been closed to missionaries, the tribes in the northern areas continue to be receptive to the gospel, and churches are multiplying there. In December, 1972, the Far East Broadcasting Company in Manila set a new record for the number of letters from a single area in a month—eight thousand letters from northern Burma. New ingatherings are also reported in Cambodia and Thailand.

Korea seems to be well on the way to becoming a Christian nation. Something like 15 percent of the population of South Korea is already Christian. Christianity is well thought of by Koreans in general, and many non-Christians there are anxious to know more about Jesus Christ. A most recent harvest has taken place in the Korean army, where over 50 percent of the army personnel has accepted Christ, and thousands have sealed their decision in the waters of baptism. The number of Christians in the army has surpassed 250,000. It is not difficult to forecast that the spread of the gospel will be accelerated when these men return to their homes with the good news.

Missions: Mickey Mouse?

When you look out there and see what God's doing, you can understand why an increasing number of Christians have stopped believing that missions is "Mickey Mouse" and have started to jump on board. Bible schools and seminaries are taking missions more seriously and adding staff and courses. Missions texts were scarce a decade ago, but great numbers are rolling off the presses now. Entire graduate schools specialize in missions. One of them, at Fuller Seminary, now offers the first Doctorate in Missiology. The American Society of Missiology was chartered in St. Louis in 1973 with over three hundred charter members.

More and more older people are saying, "Tell me more. I want to be informed." More and more young people are asking, "How can I get involved personally in the excitement of missions?" The chapters that follow are designed to answer these questions.

Now is the time to get the answers. Now is the springtime of missions.

For further reading:

Kane, J. Herbert. *A Global View of Christian Missions.* Grand Rapids: Baker Book House, 1971.

Winter, Ralph D. *The 25 Unbelievable Years 1945-1969.* South Pasadena, CA: William Carey Library, 1970.

Are the Heathen Really Lost?

CHAPTER 2

Not too far back, I mentioned that the word *heathen* is suspect these days. I still used it in the title of this chapter, however, because that's the way the question has been framed for many, many years. To a large extent, it is the key theological question for missions. If you're not satisfied that the answer is yes, you might as well forget about getting involved in missions.

The first step is to be sure we understand the question. The two key words are *heathen* and *lost*.

1. Heathen. Since this is an unfortunate word, let's update it and say that we are referring to those people in the world who have yet to accept Jesus Christ as Saviour. That helps us understand that we are talking, not just about the naked cannibals in Mamba Bamba, but also about the fourth world people in our own neighborhoods here in the United States. If he has not yet committed himself to Christ, the organic chemist is as much of a "heathen" as the cannibal.

2. Lost. Some will wonder if it is worthwhile stopping to define the word *lost*. It shouldn't be necessary, but it is. As a matter of fact, many Christian leaders seem to get increasingly confused over its meaning as time goes on.

The opposite of *lost*, of course, is *found* or *saved*. Salvation is what the lost need. Jesus came to "seek and to *save* the *lost*" (Luke 19:10). Because in recent years so many people, especially leaders in the World Council of Churches, have been asking, "What do you mean, *saved?*" or "What do you mean, *lost?*" their Commission on World Mission and Evangelism convened a major conference in Bangkok over New Year's 1972–1973 on the subject "Salvation Today." Far from clearing up the confusion, the conference only added to it.

The book that was published to prepare delegates for the conference defined lostness and salvation in every conceivable way. Frequently lostness meant suffering under social oppression, and salvation was to come through the revolution. Salvation implied freedom from torture, or humanization, or victory over enemies, suggesting also salvation from sin. But one testimony told of a man's lostness in ideology until he was "saved by Mao."

It's regrettable that so much confusion has surrounded a concept crucial for missions. It is hard to believe that for anyone God's revelation is that muddy. Why do some people want to avoid the idea that what the Bible means by salvation is, in its most profound dimension, salvation from sin and its consequences?

It's not as complex as some make it out to be.

God told Adam that the day he sinned he would die (Genesis 2:17). Adam sinned, and that day he died. The Bible explains this in its first three chapters. From Genesis 3 on, the whole human race is described as *lost* in sin, and the Bible develops the story of how God took the initiative to *save* mankind from sin and death.

Adam's death was both spiritual and physical. Spiritually, he was dead because he was from that moment alienated from God and out of fellowship with Him. Physically, he did not become an instant corpse, but from that moment on he was mortal—doomed to die physically.

Losing the Garden of Eden

But Adam's sin caused a third problem that some miss. Spiritually he lost fellowship with God, physically he lost immortality, but materially he lost the Garden of Eden. Sin produced the possibility of poverty, exploitation, war, dehumanization, social injustice, slavery, pollution, and any other social problem of yesterday or today.

As you read through the Old and New Testaments, you find that God deals with all three of these problems. Each one has many complex ramifications, and international conferences of scholars could meet to debate them. But it does seem that the general outlines of the solution emerge clearly, even to Christians who would not classify themselves as scholars.

1. The material or social problem. God made man to live in the Garden of Eden where material and social problems were unknown. Sin got him expelled and placed in the dog-eat-dog world of blood, hate, and filth. This did not please God then, nor does it please Him now. He wishes man were back in the Garden, but the cherubim with the flaming sword are there guarding the entrance (Gen. 3:24). As a matter of fact, God Himself put the cherubim there, and only He can take them away. So far, man has not returned to the Garden of Eden mainly because his sin will not allow it.

God is the Lord of the universe. He controls every aspect of the life of men and societies and nations. If He wanted to remove the cherubim and let man return to the Garden, He could do it immediately. Instead He keeps man out. By His grace, however, man is never as bad off as he could be. God chides and corrects. He sends the rain on the just and the unjust. He sends His prophets to remind man that he is mistreating his neighbor, and admonishes him to live a better life. But man outside the Garden is somewhat less than human, and he has been for *thousands* of years.

It will not always be like this. Someday man will return, not to the Garden of Eden, but to the New Jerusalem. The first book of the Bible, Genesis, tells how man was separated from the tree of life (Gen. 3:24), and the last book, Revelation, tells how he once again is restored to the tree of life (Rev. 22:2). The rest of the Bible tells of what happens in the meantime. Much does happen, but one thing that does *not* happen is the total solution of the social and material problems that have plagued man since he was punished for sin and banished from the Garden.

The final solution to man's social and material problems, caused by sin, is eschatological, meaning at the end of human history as we know it. Meanwhile, God by His grace allows and encourages partial solutions to the problems and He urges man to do the best he can in living the most human life possible. This aspect of man's responsibility is often called the "cultural mandate."

If you reread the Old Testament prophets you will see how, on page after page, they thunder forth with the cultural mandate, admonishing mankind to love his neighbor more, to put an end to oppression of other human beings, to share the wealth, to live honest lives, or, in a word, to be more human. Jesus declared Himself in the same tradition when He said that the Spirit had anointed Him to preach the gospel to the poor, heal the brokenhearted, preach deliverance to the captives, and recovering of sight to the blind, to set at liberty them that are bruised, to preach the acceptable year of the Lord. (See Luke 4:18,19.)

There is a real sense, then, in which God desires that the lot of mankind be improved. But the cherubim are still there. Their flaming swords remind us that we cannot return to the Garden of Eden, much as we wish we could. As long as human history lasts, quarreling, exploitation, sexual immorality, injustice, poverty and prejudice will be

18

a part of human life. They should remind us of the terrible consequences of sin and turn our eyes in hope toward the New Jerusalem, where the tree of life will finally heal the nations (Rev. 22:2).

2. *The physical problem.* Physical death began the moment Adam sinned, and spread to all men (Rom. 5:12). Physical death does not mean that you no longer exist after death (as in the case of animals), but it involves the separation of the body from the spirit. This is painful enough for the person whose body gets sick, wastes away, is burned, suffers an accident, or whatever else might be involved in his dying process. It is even more painful for surviving loved ones who were attached to the one taken from them.

Physical sickness and death are ugly consequences of sin. Some, however, will escape death. In the Bible we have cases such as Enoch (Gen. 5:24) and Elijah (2 Kings 2:11) who were taken without suffering physical death. When Christ comes again, the whole generation of Christians who are on earth at that time will bypass physical death and be taken directly to be with God (1 Cor. 15:52; 1 Thess. 4:17).

Jesus, of course, triumphed over death through His resurrection. He promises that some day we will all be resurrected (the unjust as well as the just), and that the "mortal must put on immortality" (1 Cor. 15:53). In other words, some day in the future we will be like Adam once again. But this will not happen until the end times, when Jesus conquers the last of all enemies, death (1 Cor. 15:24-26).

In the meantime, Jesus set the example in doing what He could to relieve physical suffering. He healed the lepers and gave sight to the blind. His disciples had power to heal and to cast out demons, and they used it. We are to do likewise as the parable of the Good Samaritan teaches us. Relieving physical suffering is another important part of the cultural mandate, along with caring for material and social problems.

3. *The spiritual problem.* The worst consequence of Adam's sin was spiritual death, the separation of man from God. God originally created Adam in His own image in order to enjoy fellowship. The instant Adam sinned, this fellowship was broken. Instead of being a friend, man became God's enemy (Rom. 5:10). Salvation was needed in the sense of reconciliation to God, and Jesus died on the cross in order to provide that reconciliation (Rom. 5:10). While we were yet sinners, Christ died for us (Rom. 5:8), and we are justified through His blood (Rom. 5:9).

These passages we have referred to from Romans 5 point out an even more frightening aspect of spiritual death. Verse 9 speaks of our being saved from *wrath.* Although many people today would like to disguise it, they cannot just wish hell away. Hell is a real place; it is a place of wrath and torment. Once in hell there is no way out, for hell is the ultimate consequence of sin.

When you think of hell—eternity apart from God with no escape whatsoever—man's other problems seem pretty small. Freedom from poverty and fear, racial brotherhood, just social structures, health and well-being—these are all important values, but none comes close to being as crucial as liberation from the wrath to come.

The solution of man's temporal problems compares to the solution of his spiritual problem like a chunk of coal to a three-karat diamond, or a mule to a Cadillac, or a slice of bread to filet mignon.

Lost? What's That?

To get back to our original question, then: What do you mean by *lost?*

Lost materially and socially? Yes.

Lost physically? Yes.

Lost spiritually? Yes, and this is the most serious of all

since it carries the possibility that man will be separated from God for eternity in hell.

When we ask: Are the heathen lost? we are essentially asking whether men and women who are not yet committed to Jesus Christ will go to hell. Without beating around the bush, the answer is yes, they will. "The wages of sin is death" (Rom. 6:23) just as it was back then in the Garden of Eden. Man sinned and died then, man sins and dies now.

This brings us to the other half of the verse just quoted (Rom. 6:23): "but the gift of God is eternal life through Jesus Christ our Lord."

We must be crystal clear on this point, because it brings us to the theological bedrock for missions. Because of sin, every man and every woman is headed for hell, but no one needs to arrive there. The difference between those who arrive and those who do not is Jesus Christ. Those who confess the Lord Jesus and believe in their heart that God raised Him from the dead will be saved (Rom. 10:9). Those who don't, will not. God does not want one person to perish (2 Peter 3:9). This is so important that the angels in heaven rejoice every time a sinner repents of his sin and trusts Jesus for salvation. (See Luke 15:10.)

There is no question as to God's desire, but how does He carry out His purpose? If He wanted to, He could appear face to face with every one of the billions of people in the fourth world, speak to him in his own language, and tell him that Christ died for his sins and that He wants to save him. If God would do this, fine, there would be no need for missions. Why He doesn't do it this way, all the theologians in Christendom don't know. All we know is that He has decided to do it in another way. He has decided to use Christian people to do it; and we accept His decision.

The only thing that will save the fourth world is faith in Jesus Christ. Romans 10 is a key passage of Scripture

21

at this point. It says that "whosoever shall call upon the name of the Lord shall be saved" (v. 13). From that point on, the logic of the passage is powerful:

How can they call on Him unless they believe in Him?

How can they believe in Jesus if they have never heard of Him?

How can they hear unless someone preaches the gospel to them?

How can anyone go and preach the gospel to them unless he is sent? In its root meaning, *missionary* means a "sent one." That is why Romans 10 is a key *missionary* passage.

God will save many of those people lost in the fourth world, but He will do it only through men and women who preach to them the gospel of Jesus Christ. This is called the "evangelistic mandate."

Sidestepping the Issue

It is so unpleasant to think of hell as real that some people have attempted to sidestep the issue. They have developed theories of missions that do not require stressing eternal life or eternal damnation. In order to keep it as simple as possible, I will call them universalists and horizontalists.

1. Universalists. The doctrine of universalism postulates that all men and women eventually will end up in heaven. Universalists reach this position from several different points of view. Some say that man really isn't as bad as all that and that he will somehow make it to heaven. Some say that even if a person does not accept Christ in this life, God will give him other chances in the future until hell is emptied. Some say that if you believe God would permit anyone to stay in hell, you cannot believe that God is love. Some say that we don't know the answer, but we do know that God is a God of grace and that His grace will eventually triumph. Some say that since Christ died on the cross for all mankind, all mankind will be saved.

Universalism is kindly. It is human. It shows deep compassion for men and women, and in this sense it reflects the love of God. But its downfall is that it is not true to the Bible. The Bible does teach that God loves the world (John 3:16) and that Christ died for the sins of the whole world (1 John 2:2). God desires that all men be saved and come to the knowledge of the truth (1 Tim. 2:4). But you cannot stop there. You cannot pick and choose which parts of the Bible you like and which you don't like. The Bible is not a divine smorgasbord. You have to take it all, not just what appeals to you.

That means you have to take seriously what Jesus said about the separation of the sheep and the goats and the everlasting fire prepared for the devil and his angels. (See Matt. 25:31-41.) Along with everlasting life, Jesus mentioned everlasting punishment (Matt. 25:46). The gospel is preached so that people will not perish (John 3:16). Those who are not written in the *Lamb's Book of Life* (in spite of the fact that they may be in the *World Christian Handbook*) will be cast into the lake of fire. (See Rev. 20:15.)

The Bible calls this the "second death," and describes it in blood-curdling terms—a lake that burns with fire and brimstone. (See Rev. 21:8.) Whether you interpret this literally or not, it can mean nothing less than horrible suffering. It is contrasted with the New Jerusalem, and *there will be people in each place for eternity.*

Universalism is not just a curiosity. Many people believe in it, but they are running away from reality and living in a dream world of their own creation. Biblical realism demands that we recognize the painful reality of hell. If we do, the missionary task of the church suddenly takes on tremendously important dimensions.

2. Horizontalists. Some horizontalists are universalists, but not all of them. Some believe all that the Bible has said, but they have come out with what I consider poorly arranged priorities.

By *horizontalism* I mean stressing the need to minister to man's horizontal needs, man-to-man and man-to-society, to the point of neglecting his vertical needs, man-to-God.

It will immediately be evident that the choices here are not either/or. As to universalism, you either believe in hell or you don't. But there is no question that man has *both* horizontal *and* vertical needs. Both need attention, not one or the other. A faithful Christian must be concerned with both. He recognizes the whole man, body and soul.

The Sliding Scale

If you were to make a sliding scale with horizontalism on the left and verticalism on the right, numbering the scale from one to ten, the first thing you would see is that anyone who placed himself at either 1.0 or 10.0 would not be deciding according to Christian principles. The 1.0 man would say, "I believe only in the cultural mandate," while the 10.0 man would say, "I believe only in the evangelistic mandate." Neither position is proper, and hardly anyone goes to such extremes.

Many people, however, approach the extremes. Some today would be over near 1.5 on the scale, for example. They believe that the supreme duty of Christian people is to act right now to relieve man's social, material, and physical suffering. They believe that salvation relates primarily to temporal lostness, not eternal lostness. Horizontalists who are also universalists would find themselves over around 1.5. You can read their writings and listen to them speak, and they never seem to be concerned about heaven and hell or the need for each man to repent of his sins, trust Jesus as his Saviour, commit himself to the body of Christ, and be saved. In fact they often ridicule this concept, saying that such "pietistic" preaching retards the battle for social justice. These are the men who advocate a moratorium on evangelism and an end to foreign missions.

Equally mistaken is the 9.5 man. He looks at people

24

as "souls with ears," and almost totally neglects the temporal needs of man. No one can take Jesus' teaching and example seriously and end up a 9.5 verticalist.

But where does the balance come? Should everybody aim for 5.0 and give equal priority to the cultural and evangelistic mandates? If not, should the scale slide slightly down toward the horizontal or should it slide up toward the vertical?

Maybe I should not answer that question, because I know in advance that some fine, Christian brethren will disagree no matter what I say. But at least I will give my opinion, because I feel that these priorities relate closely to the subject of this book and to this chapter in particular.

Setting Priorities

I feel that we ought to slide up toward the vertical end of the scale. If we err at all, it is safer to err by overstressing the vertical than by overstressing the horizontal. Why do I believe this?

Go back to the three problems caused by Adam's sin: material and social, physical, and spiritual. The material, social and physical problems all come under the *cultural mandate*. The spiritual problems come under the *evangelistic mandate*. What is God doing, and what does He intend to do about each?

1. The cultural mandate. God does not intend a total solution to material, social, or physical problems in this life. If He intended a total solution to the material and social lostness of man, He would have to remove the cherubim from the gateway to the Garden of Eden, and it looks as though He doesn't intend to do this until the New Jerusalem is ready for occupancy. If He intended a total solution to the physical lostness of man, He would banish sickness and death, but He hasn't done this, nor will He until the resurrection when the corruptible shall put on incorruption. (See 1 Cor. 15:53.)

25

In the meantime, the cultural mandate is still in effect. God wants us to do what we can to improve man's material, social, and physical condition. This is not optional; it is required of all those who wish to obey God. But let's be realistic. All that we do under the cultural mandate is penultimate, not ultimate. It is stopgap, not total.

2. The evangelistic mandate. On the other hand, God offers here and now a total solution to man's spiritual lostness. As a matter of fact, whereas material, social, and physical problems will be totally solved only in the life to come, spiritual problems can be totally solved *only* in this life. Once a man dies, his spiritual destiny has been sealed forever (Heb. 9:27). This is an ultimate, not a penultimate issue.

In other words, if you goof on the cultural mandate, it is too bad, but salvation from material, social, and physical lostness will come in the future if the ultimate problem is cared for. But if you goof on the evangelistic mandate, you've blown it forever as far as that person is concerned. He will never have fellowship with God, and therefore he will never enjoy any of the blessings of the New Jerusalem. That's why, if I make any mistake at all, I prefer to make mine up near the vertical end rather than down near the horizontal end of the scale.

Put all this together, and you see how important missions are. You understand why Jesus said, "Go and make disciples of all the nations, baptizing them in the name of the Father and the Son and the Holy Spirit" (Matt. 28:19). You see why missions are not just something for ladies on Tuesday afternoons, but that they are the very essence of total obedience to Jesus as Lord.

The heathen *are* lost. They will be lost as long as Christians fail to reach them with the good news of eternal life through Jesus.

But the lost can be found. The sheep can return to the fold. God's desire is that all be found, and if you're a

Lamb's Book of Life Christian, He wants to use you to help find them.

For further reading:

McGavran, Donald, ed. *Eye of the Storm*. Waco: Word Books, 1972.

Beyerhaus, Peter. *Missions: Which Way?* and *Shaken Foundations*. Grand Rapids: Zondervan Publishing House, 1971 and 1972.

Every Christian
Is NOT a Missionary

How often I have heard a stirring missionary message conclude with the words, "Every Christian is a missionary: if for some reason you can't go to the mission field yourself, you must send someone else in your place!"

Such a statement I classify as theological humbug!

No doubt this type of appeal has helped some Christians take missions more seriously, and this is all to the good. But the same appeal has often stimulated two other kinds of reactions that have not helped the cause of missions.

1. Some well-meaning Christians have actually gone to the mission field and washed out because they really were not missionaries to start with.

2. Some Christians have not gone to the mission field, but as a result of taking this appeal seriously, they have for many years found themselves plagued by serious and unnecessary guilt feelings, thereby losing part of their Christian joy.

If you think that every Christian is a missionary, you have not understood the precise nature of the missionary call.

If you do not understand just what the missionary call is, you have not understood the doctrine of spiritual gifts and how it applies to missions.

The purpose of this chapter is to clear up the matter, and hopefully allow you to see just where God has placed you in the total picture. It is designed to sharpen the focus on spiritual gifts and the missionary call.

God says He does not want us ignorant of spiritual gifts (1 Cor. 12:1). He wants us to:

a. know the doctrine of spiritual gifts, and

b. know exactly where each one of us fits in.

Ignorance of spiritual gifts apparently was one of the serious problems of the Corinthian church (Paul dedicated chapters 12, 13, and 14 of First Corinthians to the subject). Unfortunately, such ignorance continues to retard our churches today. Many people, however, are waking up to the need to understand and apply biblical teaching on spiritual gifts to their lives and to their churches. Among some, it is becoming a very strong emphasis, whereas a decade or two ago the same Christians may have been exceedingly timid about the subject. Even during my own seminary training in the early 1950s, several professors implied that many of the gifts had ceased at the end of the apostolic age. One reason for this attitude was that these professors, like many others, had not yet come to terms with the Pentecostal movement, which at that time had not gained the strength and acceptance it enjoys today. Some people avoided stressing spiritual gifts for fear that someone might classify them as Pentecostals.

Churches like the Peninsula Bible Church of Palo Alto, California, which has no connection at all with Pentecostalism, have been revitalized by a new and dynamic understanding of spiritual gifts. Their pastor, Ray Stedman, has written a key book on the subject called, *Body Life*. Missions like Overseas Crusades take very seriously a person's spiritual gifts in their candidate procedure as well as their

30

field placement. Leading Christian periodicals are giving more and more space to spiritual gifts and their implications in the Christian life.

In spite of these encouraging signs, there is still much ignorance of spiritual gifts.

What Spiritual Gifts Are Not

Before attempting to understand just what spiritual gifts are, it will help to clarify what they are not, particularly in two areas.

1. Spiritual gifts are not natural talents. Every member of the human race has some sort of natural talent. Your natural talent may or may not carry over and become your spiritual gift. It is common, for example, for a person who is a good teacher before he is a Christian, to find he has the spiritual gift of teaching after his conversion. But this is not *necessarily* the case.

When a person becomes a Christian and his name is written in the *Lamb's Book of Life,* he receives a spiritual gift. In other words, every Christian without exception has a spiritual gift (1 Cor. 12:7). This is natural because becoming a Christian involves becoming a member of the body of Christ, and God expects every member of the Body to function. Each Christian functions basically according to his spiritual gift.

No one has a spiritual gift *before* his conversion, although he has natural talents. Everyone has one or more gifts *after* his conversion. Of course he keeps his natural talents as well. The problem is that so few Christians realize they have a spiritual gift, and therefore they cannot use it. No wonder some of our churches are impotent. The members of the Body are not working effectively. They are suffering paralysis. Some pastors attempt to remedy the problem by souping up their church programs, but like an iron lung, this is only a temporary palliative. What is really needed for spiritual vitality is a massive awakening of Christians to their spiritual gifts.

I am convinced that enough spiritual power to win the world in our generation is now bottled up in American churches, but it will be released only when Christians realize that they are members of the Body and begin working at it.

2. *Spiritual gifts are not fruit of the Spirit.* One of the most common misstatements made by Christians is to speak of the "gift of love." Biblically, love is not classified as a spiritual gift, but rather as the fruit of the Spirit. Galatians 5:22 says, "the *fruit* of the Spirit is love, joy, peace. . . ."

You will be confused if you do not realize that, whereas not all Christians have the same *gifts,* all must produce the same *fruit,* namely love and its derivatives. This is precisely why 1 Corinthians 13, the great love chapter of the Bible, is an integral part of the great passage on gifts, 1 Corinthians 12–14. The first three verses of the chapter name several of the spiritual gifts, and go on to say that you can have the gifts, but without love (fruit), these gifts are sounding brass and a tinkling cymbal—they profit nothing (1 Cor. 13:1–3). One of the reasons the Corinthian church was in such a disastrous condition when Paul wrote was that they had all the gifts (1 Cor. 1:7), but they lacked the fruit.

Gifts and fruit are like an engine and wheels. You can have a roaring engine, but without wheels the car won't go. The wheels alone can roll downhill, but not much more. Cars need both engine and wheels. The church needs both spiritual gifts and the fruit of the Spirit.

Notice that there is no relationship between a person's sanctification (meaning his growth in grace, Christian maturity, walk with the Lord, or whatever you might call it), and the *possession* of spiritual gifts. If you are a Christian, you will have spiritual gifts whether you have much fruit of the Spirit or not. But there is a direct relationship between *effectiveness* in the use of the gifts you have and the quality of your Christian life. Only when the Holy Spirit is in control of your life can you use your gifts well.

What the Spiritual Gifts Are

The three major lists of spiritual gifts are found in 1 Corinthians 12, Romans 12, and Ephesians 4. There is a certain amount of overlapping in the lists, but each one adds something new. Put them all together, and you come out with a composite something like this:

Administration	Liberality
Apostlehood	Mercy
Discernment	Ministry
Evangelism	Miracles
Exhortation	Pastorship
Faith	Prophecy
Healing	Teaching
Helps	Tongues
Interpretation	Wisdom
Knowledge	

Of course, at this point it would be interesting to stop and define each one of these gifts, but that would take us far beyond the purpose of this book. At the moment we are basically concerned as to just where the *missionary* fits into the picture.

In order to do that, we must first notice that none of the three lists of gifts is exhaustive. There is no reason to think the composite list above is exhaustive, either. For one thing, I have found at least two other gifts that pop up outside the main lists. One is the gift of celibacy (1 Cor. 7:7), and the other the gift of martyrdom (1 Cor. 13:3).

I don't see anything wrong with suggesting that there might be some spiritual gifts in the body that were not mentioned specifically in the New Testament. A couple

33

might be intercessory prayer and hospitality, for example. Another might well be what I call the "missionary gift."

The Missionary Gift

Because of the nature of this book, we must pause here to probe the meaning of the "missionary gift." What is it that distinguishes a missionary from another member of the Body who does not have the missionary gift? As I see it, the missionary gift is the ability God gives to some members of the Body to minister in a different culture.

The missionary gift should not be confused with the gift of apostlehood or the gift of evangelism. They are sometimes identified erroneously, but they are three different things. The apostle is one who has particular authority in the church at large, and he is sent out in a broad ministry. He is often an evangelist, and he is often a teacher. But in order to be an apostle, he doesn't have to minister in a second culture. Peter is an example of an apostle who was not a missionary. True, he went to Cornelius' home, but he went only because of a special directive from God, not because he had the missionary gift.

Paul, on the other hand, was an apostle who did have the missionary gift and who used his apostolic gift in a second culture. This is brought out in Ephesians 3 where Paul speaks of himself as the prisoner of Jesus Christ for the Gentiles (3:1). He was a Hebrew through and through (Acts 22:3; 23:6), and to identify closely with pork-eating Gentiles was not at all natural for him. But Paul says he was made a minister to the Gentiles "according to the gift of the grace of God" (Eph. 3:7). He emphasizes that his ability to preach to the Gentiles was from the "grace given" (Eph. 3:8), which gains meaning when we realize that the word *grace* is synonymous with *spiritual gift*. (See Rom. 12:6.)

In other words, Paul's spiritual gift enabled him to minister in another culture. I call this, in modern terminology

34

(since *missionary* is not a biblical word), the *missionary gift*. The best statement of it is in 1 Corinthians 9:22 where Paul says, "I am made all things to all men, that I might by all means save some." Not everyone can do it. Peter, for example, couldn't. That's why Paul says clearly, "the gospel of the uncircumcision (Gentiles) was committed unto me, as the gospel of the circumcision (Jews) was unto Peter" (Gal. 2:7). If we adopt the hypothesis of the missionary gift, all these pieces fall into place.

Some missionaries are evangelists, some are not. The ones who are simply have two gifts, meaning that they lead others to Christ (as an evangelist) in a second culture (as a missionary). Most evangelists use their gifts in their own culture because they do not have the gift of being a missionary to go along with it.

The Missionary Call

By this time, it is clearer than ever that not all Christians are missionaries. In fact, more Christians are not missionaries than are, just as more members of your body are not fingers than are. The whole body can't be one 150-pound eye (1 Cor. 12:17). It would make just about as much sense to say that every Christian is a pastor, which hardly anyone ever says. The Corinthians went off the track in a similar way by saying that every Christian should have the gift of tongues (1 Cor. 14).

What is the missionary call, then? To come right to the point, there is no difference between the missionary *call* and the missionary *gift*. As a matter of fact, there is no difference between any call and the corresponding gift. God never gives a spiritual gift to a member of the Body without "calling" him to use that gift as it should be used in the Body. Moreover, God never "calls" a person to a task in the body of Christ without equipping him with the gift needed to do the task. The call implies the gift, and vice versa. If you have the missionary gift, you have

35

a missionary call, and you will do well to obey the call and use the gift.

Gift and Role

We have already distinguished between gifts and natural talents and between gifts and fruit. At this point it will help to distinguish between gifts and *role*.

If you go back over the list of spiritual gifts, you will notice that several of them do not seem to describe anything special at all. They simply name things that all Christians have or do.

Take, for example, the gift of faith. What Christian doesn't have faith? But when you examine it a little closer, you find that there are at least three kinds of faith mentioned in the New Testament.

1. Saving faith. "By grace are ye saved through *faith;* and that not of yourselves: it is the gift of God" (Eph. 2:8). When a person becomes a Christian he receives the gift of saving faith. Therefore every Christian has this kind of faith, but it is not to be confused with the other kinds.

2. Faith as fruit of the Spirit. "The fruit of the Spirit is love, joy, peace, longsuffering, gentleness, goodness, *faith.* . . ." (Gal. 5:22). Every Christian's life should be characterized by a constant attitude of faith, produced by the presence of the Holy Spirit. This kind of faith is what I call a *role,* something expected of every Christian. In that sense it is different from a *gift.*

3. The gift of faith (1 Cor. 12:9). As in the case of other gifts, some Christians have a special ability to exercise faith that other Christians don't have. In one place it is described as "faith . . . to remove mountains" (1 Cor. 13:2). George Mueller of Bristol is a well-known model of someone with this gift.

Giving or liberality (Rom. 12:8) is another example of the difference between gift and role. Giving is not an optional activity for a Christian. Every Christian is expected

36

to give to the Lord's work as a matter of course. In fact, it is my opinion that if you give less than 10 percent of your income you are robbing God. You are not fulfilling your *role*. But over and above that, some Christians have a remarkable *gift* of liberal giving. One Christian businessman with this gift used to donate 90 percent of his income to God's work, and then tithe his own 10 percent! As every fully supported missionary knows, such people are crucial in God's kingdom, but it is not expected that every Christian can or will give that large a proportion of his income. Only those with the gift of liberality can do it properly.

The confusion behind the statement, "every Christian is a missionary" can be further clarified at this point. I suspect that what is really meant is that every Christian is a witness or an ambassador. This is true enough. Every Christian has the *role* of a witness for Christ (Acts 1:8), but every Christian does not have the *gift* of being an evangelist (Eph. 4:11), much less the *gift* of being a missionary.

The Gifts and the Body

If you check it out, you'll notice that in every one of the three Bible passages where a major list of spiritual gifts appears (1 Cor. 12, Rom. 12, and Eph. 4) Paul uses the analogy of the body. Instead of simply saying that "Christians are members of the church," he puts it much more graphically: "Christians are members of the body of Christ." This is good. Back then not many people knew what the Church was. Today too many people may know what it is, and some have consequently developed weird ideas as to just what the Church is and what its members are supposed to do.

But the human body is the same now as it was then, and the average person has about the same basic knowledge of the body and its members. You don't have to be able

37

to describe cloning or have a Ph.D. in anatomy to understand how hands, eyes, veins, knees, and skin relate to each other in daily life. The analogy spans time and cultures. Eskimo teeth are used to masticate food just like Korean or Arab teeth. Breasts nourish babies from Argentina to Zaire. When you ask almost any human being to think of Christians as members of the Body, he can follow the analogy easily.

With a minimum of explanation, he will understand that the body is one organism. In three ways, this is particularly related to the Church:

1. The body has one head. The brain controls the central nervous system and provides direction and coordination to the whole body. In this sense, Christ is the head of the body of Christ (Eph. 4:15-16). Regardless of the gifts he has, no Christian should get the idea that he is head of the Body. Jesus is.

2. The body has one blood. Every cell of the human body receives nourishment from the same blood. The drop of blood that feeds the calf of my leg this time might feed my ear lobe the next time around. The body of Christ is also nourished by one blood. Every true Christian has been brought into the Body through the blood of Christ (Eph. 1:7), and no other way.

3. The body has one spirit. Man's soul or spirit is unconfined. The same spirit is in your thumb or your bone marrow or your gall bladder. It cannot be isolated into one member only. By the same token, the Holy Spirit is in every member of the body of Christ (Rom. 8:9).

These three powerful factors unify the body; nevertheless the members differ one from another. How do they get there? The Bible clearly says that they are placed there by the Holy Spirit Himself (1 Cor. 12:11,18). Every Christian's spiritual gift makes him a particular member of the Body, and that gift is given to him entirely by God's choice. It is a mistake to think that God gives us a celestial order blank with a list of the gifts and asks us to check off the ones we would like best. Some verses that could sound like that (such as "covet earnestly the best gifts" or "desire spiritual gifts" as in 1 Cor. 12:31 and 14:1) refer, not to the individual Christian, but to the Church in general. No other person, whether pastor or teacher or archbishop, can pass out spiritual gifts to fellow Christians. God uses men and women to do some things for Him, but this task is not one of them. He does it "as He will" (1 Cor. 12:11).

The reason for this is that the worldwide Church is such a complex organism that only God Himself has a broad enough grasp of the Church and its needs to distribute the gifts properly. Since God is in charge, it does not seem possible that any church would lack the gifts it needs to function in a healthy and vital way. Sick and ineffective churches probably do not lack the gifts; their members simply are not using them as they should.

Just as God gives different gifts to different people, He also gives different combinations of gifts to different churches. This is why I don't get nervous just because my own local church does not have exactly the same gifts as the church down the street. God knows what gifts each of us needs to function properly. But in spite of this diversity, gifts must be used together, coordinated by the Head. Jesus must be fully in charge. My foot is working well now, but if I cut it off and put it over on the couch, it might still be my foot (no one else would claim it!), but it is of no use to me because the head could no longer control it.

All members of the Body need each other. Pretend you see a peanut vendor down the street. Now make a list of every member of your body that you need in order to buy a sack of peanuts, eat one, and nourish your body with its protein. That's why Paul says, "the eye cannot say unto the hand, I have no need of thee. . . ." (1 Cor. 12:21). No matter what my own gifts are, they are useless unless they are working with other members of the Body.

Where You Fit In

So much for what could be called the biblical doctrine of spiritual gifts. But as I mentioned previously, not only does God want us to know the doctrine, He also wants us to know how each one of us fits into the practical working out of the doctrine.

This practical side is vitally important to every Christian because it relates so closely to the final judgment. It is no news that some day each Christian is going to appear before Christ for His judgment. (See 2 Cor. 5:10.) Some will be called "good and faithful servants," but others will be "wicked and slothful servants," according to the parable in Matthew 25:14-30.

What will be the basis of judgment? Obviously, what you and I did with what God entrusted to us. He entrusts many things to us to use in this life, but nothing is more important than the spiritual gifts He gives us. To a large extent, then, we will be judged according to how we function as members of the body of Christ during our life here on earth. A Christian who doesn't take the time, effort, and prayer necessary to be sure of his own particular gift or gifts cannot prepare himself very well for the judgment. That is one reason why God does not want us ignorant of spiritual gifts (1 Cor. 12:1).

Notice the vital relationship between the judgment verse (2 Cor. 5:10) and the major spiritual gift passage (Rom. 12). Second Corinthians says we will be judged according to what we did in our *bodies,* good or bad. Romans says we must present our *bodies,* a living sacrifice. How do we do this, proving the good, acceptable, and perfect will of God? Romans 12:1,2 are only the introductory verses to the passage that follows on the body and the gifts (Rom. 12:3-8).

In order to please God, I need to know what my gift

is, or as Paul says, I need to "think soberly, according as God hath dealt to every man the measure of faith" (Rom. 12:3). I must avoid the extremes of being either too proud or too humble, and I must go through whatever spiritual exercise is necessary in order to come to an accurate and realistic conclusion as to what gift God has given me and to what degree I have it. On that basis, I live my Christian life and function as a member of the body of Christ.

Know What Your Gift Isn't

Just as important as knowing what gift God *has* given you is knowing which gifts He *hasn't* given you. Many Christians try for years to function with gifts they never had in the first place, and this doesn't do the Lord's work much good. It's like trying to hear something with your knee or throw a ball with your nose. Knees and noses are better off doing other things.

No one told me this while I was in seminary, and consequently, when I first went to Bolivia as a missionary, I had the idea that I wanted to be an evangelist like Billy Graham. But after some time I became concerned that, in spite of well-constructed and thoroughly biblical evangelistic sermons, when I gave the invitation no one would come! For a long time I worried that I wasn't praying enough, or that some sin in my life was standing between me and God, or that I needed more of the Holy Spirit or the deeper life. I worked on these problems diligently, but to no avail. I still gave invitations and nobody came! Personal evangelism produced similar results, and very few came to Christ through my evangelistic ministry.

Whenever I thought of Billy Graham, I became more and more frustrated. When he held out his arms and said, "Come!" multitudes came. I held out *my* arms almost in vain.

Then the Lord showed me what I am now sharing about

41

spiritual gifts. Among other things, He showed me that I did not have the gift of evangelism. This was a turning point in my Christian life. Frustrations and guilt lifted like the morning mist. I began to feel a joy in serving Christ I had not experienced before. I now know that I am not another Billy Graham. God has given him the gift of evangelism, but He has not given it to me. I still receive occasional invitations to preach evangelistic crusades, but I turn them down without hesitation. Life is too short to squander my energies attempting to be something I now know I am not.

Let me hasten to add that I still have a *role* as a witness, and I try to be faithful in this. God occasionally gives me the privilege of leading a soul to Christ, and when I do it is a red-letter day for me. But I also realize that the *role* of a witness is not the same as the *gift* of an evangelist.

I have tried other gifts, such as the gift of pastor, with a similar lack of results. On the positive side, God has showed me what gifts I *do* have. I have three in particular: teacher, administrator, and missionary, and I spend a very large part of my waking hours using these three gifts with all the vigor I can muster. When the time comes for the judgment, Jesus is not going to ask me what I have done with the gifts of an evangelist or a pastor, since He never gave them to me. But He *is* going to ask me what I did as a teacher, administrator, and missionary, and I want to be ready for His questions.

If you come to "think soberly of yourself" in this light, you will avoid three very common spiritual pitfalls:

1. *False pride.* Since God is the one who assigns the gifts and consequent functions as a member of the Body, your gift is in no way of your own making. You have no reason at all to be proud of it or to consider yourself superior to any other person (or, member of the Body).

2. *False humility.* If you carry the Christian virtue of

humility too far, you may find yourself saying, "I am just a tiny member of the Body, and my gifts don't amount to much. Others may be giants, but I am satisfied to be a nobody." Result: You think you have no gift, and you do nothing. This false humility is detrimental to your own life and to the Body as a whole. Just be honest and realistic about what God has given you, and don't be afraid to admit you have a gift.

3. *Envy.* When you look around, there will be others who *do* appear to be giants. God has placed each one in his proper place, however, and this includes you. God wants you happy with the gift you have, happy with the gifts others have, and happy to be able to work together for His glory. Just the thought of an eyelid envying a fingernail because they do different things is ridiculous.

How to Find Your Gift

By now, you may agree with me that one of the most important spiritual exercises that a Christian can possibly undertake is a sincere and relentless search for his own spiritual gift or gifts. To conclude this chapter, I will suggest five steps that you should take to do this. If you get a positive response to all five, you can be reasonably sure that you have the gift involved.

1. *Explore the options.* Know what the gifts are and what they imply. This chapter has been a starter, particularly for the missionary gift. Study well 1 Corinthians 12, Romans 12, and Ephesians 4.

2. *Experiment with as many as possible.* You won't be able to try out every gift on the list, but you can try many, as I tried the gifts of pastor and evangelist. To try out the missionary gift you can become involved in a summer missions program, short-term missionary service, or a cross-cultural involvement in your own country.

3. *Examine your own feelings* about the gift you are experimenting with. I believe that God wants happy Chris-

tians, and that if He has given you a gift, He will give you unusual joy when you are using it. You ought to feel better about being able to use your gift than you do about almost any other activity you can think of.

4. Evaluate your effectiveness. Your gift should accomplish what it was intended for. If you are a teacher, others will learn. If you are an evangelist, others will come to Christ. This is just as natural as expecting your nose to smell.

5. Expect confirmation from the Body. If you have the gift, others in the Body will recognize it. This is essential, since every gift must be used with the other members. Ordination to the ministry is one way a gift is validated, but fellow Christians should confirm every gift, not just that of pastor. There are no Lone Rangers when it comes to spiritual gifts.

Once you find your gift, take all the time necessary to *(a)* develop the gift, and *(b)* use the gift. If you do this, without forgetting that it must be used in combination with the fruit of the Spirit, you can expect to hear "Well done, thou good and faithful servant" on that final day.

For further reading:

Stedman, Ray C. *Body Life.* Glendale: Regal Books, 1972.

Wagner, C. Peter, *A Turned-on Church in an Uptight World.* Grand Rapids: Zondervan Publishing House, 1971.

How the Machinery of Missions Runs

It is estimated that every year $350 million is spent on missions by people in the United States.

This substantial enterprise is supported almost entirely by voluntary contributions from Christians. Millions of Americans support the missionary work of the church, but relatively few understand how these missions work, what the different options are, and how they can track their dollars to see if they are accomplishing the intended goals.

Are Missions an Afterthought?

The word missions is commonly used in two senses. It often means the "missionary enterprise" of the church as a whole, or the composite of the efforts that Christians make to spread the gospel of Christ throughout the world. This is the most general meaning of the word.

It can also mean more specifically "missionary organizations," or groups which have been formed in one way or another as agencies for carrying out the larger missionary enterprise. When I raise the question, "Are missions an afterthought?" I mean missions in this organizational sense.

Mission agencies have now become a primary instrument

for world evangelization, as we will see. But before describing some of the details as to their machinery, we need to feel comfortable about their existence. Some people believe that missionary agencies are abnormal. They say that not missions, but the churches themselves, are the instruments God really wants to use for extending His kingdom. One recent writer calls the development of autonomous missionary societies an "unfortunate and abnormal historic development." Some look at missionary societies as warts on the fair skin of the church, and the sooner we can remove them the better.

I disagree!

I see missions as intrinsically related to the church—not as abnormalities, but rather as legs are related to the body.

In one sense the word *church* is so general that it includes everything we are talking about. The Church universal (sometimes called the "invisible church") includes every Christian and every group of Christians on the earth. In that sense, local churches, missionary societies, summer Bible camps, theological seminaries, Bible societies, and whatever other Christian activity you might name are all part of the Church. This is correct, but it is not very helpful at this point.

What we mean specifically by *church* is a particular, visible organization. It could be a local church, an association of churches, a whole denomination like the United Presbyterian Church, or even a state church like the Anglican Church in England.

There are some notable exceptions to the rule, but throughout history churches *as churches* have not been overly effective instruments for carrying the gospel to the regions beyond. The best success in world evangelism has usually come from situations in which the church or churches have permitted, encouraged, and supported the formation of specialized *missionary agencies* to do their missionary work.

46

The Roman Catholic church learned this lesson through the centuries. Those of our ancestors who inhabited the forests of northern Europe were largely won to Christ through missionaries working in what is called the monastic movement. The Benedictine order was founded around A.D. 500 and it was influential through Augustine of Canterbury in the conversion of England. The Franciscans, founded in the thirteenth century, sent missionaries to China and many other parts of the world. While the missionary movement of the churches of the Protestant Reformation was zero in the sixteenth century, the Jesuit order was formed in France to carry Christianity throughout the world. Today, 75 percent of Roman Catholic missionary work is done by the orders and only 25 percent by the local clergy. Of 7,176 Catholic missionaries sent out from the U.S. in 1972, only 244 or 3.5% were sent out by dioceses.

One of Martin Luther's blind spots was that he reacted so strongly against the corrupt aspects of the monastic movement (he belonged to the Augustinian Order) that he failed to appreciate what they were doing well. It did not occur to him to reform Catholic *missions* while he was reforming the Catholic *church.* So the Protestant Reformation movement ended up all church and no mission. There is no doubt that Luther himself desired that the gospel should be carried throughout the whole earth. Luther sharpened the missionary *message,* but with all his brilliance he never came clear on missionary *structures.* He was primarily a theologian and a churchman, not a missionary.

Using missions for the spread of the gospel seems to have been God's plan all along. The model for missionary societies is the Pauline band, formed in Antioch and used to carry the Christian message to many parts of the world in the first century. Acts 13 describes its organization. A certain group of Christians in the Antioch Church felt called by the Holy Spirit to move out with the gospel. The church encouraged this and sent out Paul and Barnabas as missionaries.

Paul's missionary band increased in number as the years went by, and from the data we have it seems that Paul himself functioned as the general director and coordinator. He reported back to Antioch from time to time, just as he reported to Jerusalem and other churches. The church in Philippi most likely was a heavy financial supporter of the mission. But the missionary society was not controlled by Antioch or Jerusalem or Philippi, so far as we can determine. The church was the church, and the mission was the mission, right from the beginning.

The great Protestant missionary movement began only when the heirs of Luther, Calvin, and Zwingli stumbled onto the importance of the missionary society. This happened as one of the results of the great Evangelical Awakening of the 1700s led by John and Charles Wesley and George Whitefield. Missionary societies were not unknown, since the Society for the Propagation of the Gospel in Foreign Parts had been founded in England in 1701, but that group was interested largely in ministry to British citizens overseas. The real turning point came in the years 1795-1815 when scores of what were called "voluntary associations" were formed. One of the models for these was the Baptist Missionary Society, which came into being in 1792 through the vision of William Carey, now known as the "father of modern missions." First in the United States was the American Board of Commissioners for Foreign Missions, which Congregationalists and others established in New England in 1810.

Once missionary societies gained strength, wonderful things began to happen. More men and women have been led to Christ and more Christian churches have been planted in the world in the 180 years since William Carey than in the 1800 previous years all put together. Missions are not an afterthought to God. They are an integral part of His plan for "making disciples of all nations."

Missions are not warts on the church, they are legs. The body can survive without legs, but it can't get around well. The church can survive without missions (as the churches of the Reformation did), but they can't do a good job in proclaiming Christ's name throughout the world. Legs move the body, and the body nourishes and sustains the legs. Missions move the church out, and the church in turn sustains missions. As legs are distinct, yet a part of the body, so missions are a part of the church—but don't confuse their specific functions.

What Missionary Societies Look Like

Missiologists use the word *modality* to describe the church, which includes entire families regardless of age or sex. *Sodality* in turn describes the voluntary association that only those particularly interested in the stated task of the group join and participate in. Modalities and sodalities are not mutually exclusive: they need each other. Catholic orders such as the Jesuits and Maryknoll Fathers are sodalities, but they operate within one modality, the Catholic Church. The Anglican Church also has such mission sodalities as the Church Missionary Society or the South America Missionary Society. The World Mission Prayer League is a Lutheran sodality that relates to several different Lutheran groups in the U.S.A. The Sudan Interior Mission is another type of sodality, relating to churches of all denominations, but almost exclusively to those of evangelical persuasion. Some modalities such as the United Presbyterian Church have discouraged the formation of sodalities; they prefer to run their mission program through a church agency called the Commission on Ecumenical Mission and Relations.

A less scientific, but more common, terminology to describe certain kinds of missions is denominational and interdenominational. The members of a *denominational mission* come from the same denomination, and when they go to the mission field they plant churches of that denomination. Examples are the Southern Baptist Foreign Mission Board, Assemblies of God Foreign Missions Department, and the World Division of Board of Mission of the United Methodist Church.

Interdenominational missions get their support from a variety of sources, recruit members without regard to their denominational affiliation, and often form a new, local denomination when they successfully plant churches on the mission field. Three of the largest interdenominational missions are Wycliffe Bible Translators, Sudan Interior Mission, and The Evangelical Alliance Mission (TEAM). Although Baptists and Presbyterians alike work with the Sudan Interior Mission, for example, their churches in Nigeria are called the Evangelical Church of West Africa (ECWA), which is neither Baptist nor Presbyterian.

Associations of Missions

Although some giant missions like the Southern Baptists (budget: $30 million per year), Wycliffe Bible Translators (total personnel: 3,000), and New Tribes Mission have chosen not to join any of the major associations of missions in the United States, most of the missions have. About two-thirds of the American missionary force is affiliated with five associations of missions:*

1. Division of Overseas Ministries, National Council of Churches. Generally speaking, the DOM brings together what are known as the mainline denominations. It has a membership of thirty-two missions representing about eight thousand missionaries.

2. Interdenominational Foreign Mission Association. Organized in 1917, the IFMA brings together forty-four inter-

---

*The text is describing the Protestant missionary force. According to the United States Catholic Mission Council, the total number of Catholic missionaries from the U.S. for 1972 was 7,649.

denominational mission boards, all evangelical in persuasion, representing roughly sixty-five hundred missionaries.

3. *Evangelical Foreign Missions Association.* Affiliated with the National Association of Evangelicals, the EFMA includes mostly denominational missions, but several interdenominational missions also hold membership, some jointly with IFMA. The membership totals sixty-three missions, representing about seventy-five hundred missionaries.

The IFMA and the EFMA work closely together on many projects, and are presently cooperating in five joint committees. One of them, Evangelical Missions Information Service, publishes the influential journal, *Evangelical Missions Quarterly.*

4. *The Associated Missions of the International Council of Christian Churches.* TAM represents nine missions, with a total missionary force of about two hundred. Its members are generally congenial to the leadership of Carl McIntire.

5. *The Fellowship of Missions.* The five members of the FOM are fundamentalist in outlook, and their missionary force totals about nine hundred with a cumulative budget of over $9 million. Some modalities, such as the General Association of Regular Baptists, do not run their own denominational missionary program, but have approved these five mission sodalities (which include Baptist Mid-Missions and the Association of Baptists for World Evangelism) as their official missionary arms, or to follow the previous analogy, their legs.

The general trend at the present time is for an increase in the number of missionaries associated with IFMA, EFMA, and FOM, while the DOM missionary force is decreasing. Data on TAM is confusing due to frequent internal reshuffling.

A Variety of Functions

Most missions are in the business of preaching the gospel,

bringing men and women to a commitment to Christ, and planting Christian churches wherever they go. It is fitting that the majority do this, as we will argue in chapter 6, since the evangelistic mandate is primary in missions. But other kinds of missions have been formed for other objectives:

1. *Service missions.* Some missions specialize in certain tasks, which they perform to aid a wide variety of other missions, but they themselves do not specialize in evangelism and church planting. Mission Aviation Fellowship, for example, provides air transportation for scores of missions that are in no position to operate their own flying program. Daystar Communications offers technical training in communications to church leaders around the world. Gospel Recordings presses and distributes records carrying evangelistic messages in hundreds of vernacular languages. The United Bible Societies translate, print and distribute the Scriptures in multiple languages. The list could go on and on.

2. *Fund-raising Agencies.* The Fuller Evangelistic Association is an example of an agency that raises funds and in turn uses them to support well-screened evangelistic missionary projects worldwide. Christian people who do not have firsthand contact with missions as such often welcome the opportunity to channel their stewardship funds through such organizations whose missiological expertise they trust. The Christian Nationals' Evangelism Commission specializes in raising funds for the support of carefully selected national church leaders in the Third World.

Some missions combine these functions. World Vision International, for example, conducts a massive fund-raising program. Some of these funds are contributed to projects administered by other missions, while some of them are used in financing World Vision's own social service projects, such as Korean orphans or a hospital in Cambodia. But World Vision also has more direct missionary involvement,

such as mass evangelistic crusades in Cambodia and outstanding pastors' conferences for Christian workers in a
great variety of nations in Asia, Africa, and Latin America.

Where Does All the Money Come From?

The $350 million that Americans spend yearly on mis-
sions comes almost entirely from voluntary contributions.
Fortunately, the U.S. government, unlike the Australian
government, for example, allows contributions to accredited
missionary organizations to be deducted from taxable income. This increases incentive, but still missions across the
board have to struggle to raise their operating funds.

Some do this quite successfully. Southern Baptists have
by far the largest missionary budget in the country, over
$30 million. Three DOM missions follow them, fitting
approximately into the $15 million to $20 million bracket:
United Methodists, Seventh-Day Adventists, and United
Presbyterians. EFMA missions in the $5 million to $10
million bracket include Assemblies of God, World Vision,
Christian and Missionary Alliance, and Church of the
Nazarene. The only two IFMA missions as high as $5
million are The Evangelical Alliance Mission and the
Sudan Interior Mission.

Most missions spend most of their income in supporting
field missionaries. The rule of thumb is to keep expenses
of the home operation at less than 20 percent of the total
budget, although some situations that involve fewer field
missionaries will not permit this. Generally speaking, missions receive funds under one of two systems:

1. *Budgetary support.* Large denominations, which finance their own boards of missions, often request their
member churches to build into their local budgets annual
grants to the board of missions of the denomination. In
such cases, most funds are undesignated, and the people
in the churches trust the mission board to allocate the funds
competently. The missionaries themselves cooperate by

keeping the churches informed as to what is happening on the field, but they do not have to be concerned with personal fund raising once they are accepted for missionary service.

2. *Personalized support.* All interdenominational missions, and many denominational missions as well, prefer the personalized system. Under this system, the missionary is responsible for raising personal support, as well as additional funds for individual and mission projects on the field. This obviously puts pressure on the missionary, but it pays off in other ways. The donors, for example, are not giving just to "foreign missions," but to a particular missionary. They know the family personally. They pray for them regularly. They receive and read letters from the field. They watch the mission magazine for a word about the work of *their* missionary. Missionaries visit periodically on "deputation." To a much larger degree, the donors back home feel personally involved in the investment of their missionary dollars.

For many years it was not considered proper for missionaries to let other people know about their financial situation. They were only to pray, tell God of their needs, and trust God to lay the needs on the hearts of His people. This silent indirect approach is often traced to Hudson Taylor, who founded the China Inland Mission (now Overseas Missionary Fellowship) in 1865. In contemporary America, however, it is becoming passé, since most American donors prefer a more straightforward and businesslike approach. But the terminology has continued, and as a result missions that depend on personalized support are still widely known as "faith missions."

Dividing the Pie

Missions receiving budgetary support generally pay salaries and fringe benefits to their missionaries. They give them travel allowances, educational grants for their children, medical plans, and cost-of-living adjustments. The missionaries are treated much as a General Motors employee in a foreign country would be treated, except at a considerably lower salary.

Personalized support missions, however, cannot manage finances in the same way. Income will fluctuate depending on the success of workers in their fund-raising ministries. Since the individual missionaries are the ones who bring in the money, they naturally feel a little more concerned with how the pie is divided. Personalized support missions disburse their funds in one of two ways:

1. *The individualized support system.* Some missions, like Wycliffe Bible Translators and the New Tribes Mission, allow each missionary to have a large control over the funds he raises. All funds designated for his support or his work go directly to him, less a deduction of something like 10 percent for home office expenses. After he subtracts an amount stipulated by the mission for his family's support, he in turn decides what aspect of the work the balance should be spent on. Sometimes a group of missionaries on a field will make joint decisions for the expenditure of some of their work funds. But all missionaries must spend these funds according to guidelines established by the U.S. Internal Revenue Service and keep close track of them. If they do not, the tax-exempt status of their mission is in jeopardy.

You can see that this system has the advantage of putting the money where the work is—out on the front lines. It also keeps pressure on the missionaries, for if their funds fall below the recommended support level, not only do they have nothing for their work, but their salary is cut accordingly. Under this system some missionaries in the same mission handle much more money than others do.

2. *The pool system.* In order to maintain more equity, some missions have developed the pool system. All funds raised by all missionaries (with the exception of designated

work funds) go into the mission pool. Mission leadership then decides, month by month, how the pool is to be spent. One of the first items, of course, is salary, but every worker receives the same amount, with adjustments for size of family. The General Director gets the same amount as the newly-arrived language school student. Decisions as to general expenses, or as to what project should be funded when, are made by the mission leadership, not by each individual.

How Missions Are Governed

The most common pattern of missionary government begins with a mission board of one kind or another here in the sending country. When the board is a modality, the church's hierarchy usually selects its members in some way. When the board is a sodality, a voluntary agency, it is a self-perpetuating board of directors, ordinarily chartered under the laws of one of the fifty states.

The board usually appoints a General Director who sets up an office in the U.S.A., meets regularly with the board, and runs the mission. He is assisted by a group of representatives at home who recruit missionaries and raise funds. On the other end, he relates to the field director of each field and travels to visit the fields as much as possible. The final authority lies in the home board, however, and the degree of control of the home over the field varies greatly from mission to mission.

Some missions, however, have their board of directors on the field, and the board consists mostly of field workers. The Overseas Missionary Fellowship and the Andes Evangelical Mission are examples of field-governed missions. Their General Director is typically a field man, and they establish home *councils* (not boards) in the sending countries to handle mission affairs there. This pattern is most common with international missions, which employ missionaries from a variety of sending countries.

On the field, the workers usually gather in an annual field conference for spiritual nourishment and to transact mission business. The business agenda depends on the structure of the conference, but one almost universal item is the election of a field council and other officers.

Although there are infinite variations to these basic patterns, mission government is usually not complex. Responsible missions are very conscientious in keeping overhead down, so that the maximum part of each dollar can be used on the field where the missionary work really is being done.

This is how the machinery runs. What specifically it intends to accomplish, we will discuss in chapter 6. Before that, though, let's take a look at the responsibility of the home churches.

For further reading:

North American Protestant Ministries Overseas Directory, compiled by MARC (Monrovia, CA: World Vision, 1970).

Winter, Ralph D. and Beaver, R. Pierce. *The Warp and the Woof.* South Pasadena, CA: William Carey Library, 1970.

They Can't Go
If They're Not Sent

The word *missionary* comes from a Latin root that means "to send." Besides having what we called the *missionary gift* in chapter 3, a true missionary is one who is *sent* to minister in another culture. This is why a British pastor, called to serve in an American church, is not considered a missionary as such. He has been *called* by the church in America, not *sent* by the church or mission in England.

This emphasis on sending comes out clearly in Romans 10, a passage we mentioned in chapter 2. There we stressed "How shall they hear without a preacher?" Here we will stress the important phrase, "How shall they preach, except they be *sent?*" (Rom. 10:15).

In the final analysis, missions begin in the home churches. From the time the first missionaries went out from the church at Antioch, the home church has been a key factor in the spread of Christianity throughout the world. If it weren't for the churches, there simply would be no missions.

Churches Nourish Missions

One of the emphases of the last chapter was that missions relate to churches as legs relate to the body. That chapter explained how the *legs* operate; this one will deal more with the *body's* role. The body nourishes and sustains the legs. The church nourishes and sustains the mission.

Obviously, missionaries are first of all members of churches. Although there are exceptions, the proper function of the church, as the body of Christ, is to help each member find and use his spiritual gifts, and this naturally includes the members with the missionary gift. Almost everyone who has been called to be a missionary can trace some of the roots of that call back to his local church. It is true that some discover their gift in a great missionary conference like the Inter-Varsity Conference held every three years at Urbana, Illinois, or in a Bible study group, or at a Christian college, or perhaps while traveling abroad. But even in these cases, when the whole story is told, the home church has usually played an important part.

Thus the first major, and essential, contribution that home churches make to missions is to supply the personnel. Churches that build an adequate missionary emphasis into their regular teaching and program find that a steady stream of their people move out to the mission fields of the world. Not everybody in the church goes, of course. The whole body isn't an eye (1 Cor. 12:17), nor does everyone have the missionary gift. Year after year, a good, missionary-minded church may find about 5 percent of its members out on the mission fields at any given time. If your church has no missionary at all, this may say something about the health of your church in general.

The Blessing of Sending

Providing the missionaries, of course, is only the beginning. As the Bible says, they must be *sent*. Sending missionaries out is expensive, complicated, and time-consum-

60

ing. But no part of the Christian life is more rewarding. An unwritten rule in the kingdom of God is that the church that is doing its part in world missions is the church that God is blessing in every conceivable way.

One of the churches that supported me and my family throughout our missionary career came up against a severe financial crisis some years ago. The official board of the church called an emergency meeting, and all knew ahead of time that something unusual had to be done if the church was not to be shipwrecked financially. Soon after the meeting began, the pastor said, "Gentlemen, I have been praying a good deal about our situation. I think the Lord has spoken to me about a solution. As a way out of our financial problem, would you consider raising our missionary budget?"

Some would have considered this a reckless and irresponsible proposal. Financially, it made no sense at all. But spiritually it did, and on the premise that God would take care of His church if it continued faithful in spreading the gospel throughout the world, the deacons and trustees decided to step out on faith and try it. It worked! The entire church budget soon went into the black, and as far as I have heard has been there ever since. This is the kind of faith that God honors.

Once the church decides to do its part in the missionary task, it needs to adopt certain policies. These policies should be based on up-to-date knowledge of how missions operate and clear thinking on missionary strategy and the role of the church. A large amount of Christian good will goes down the drain each year because churches base their missionary programs on inadequate information, stick to outmoded policies, or otherwise squander their resources. Good will is not enough. One of the purposes of this chapter is to suggest some guidelines that will lead churches to establish sound and effective missionary policies.

The "Tin Cup Complex"

A friend of mine, who served many years as a missionary and is now a pastor, recently wrote an article with the provocative title, "Let's Banish Missionary Begging." He clearly sees both sides of the coin and gives some sound advice. Surveys have shown that one of the most distasteful aspects of missionary service, particularly for young people today, is fund raising. I call it the "tin cup complex."

Churches do well to reduce the tin cup complex for missionaries as much as possible. It should not be the case, but it is painfully true that some young people today staunchly refuse missionary service, not because they lack the gift, but because they refuse to "rattle a tin cup." This is only one of the reasons why each church needs to make whatever adjustment is necessary in order to establish well-defined missionary financial policies.

Reducing the tin cup complex does not mean that missionaries should no longer be dependent on churches. It may mean that in some cases the missionary will be more dependent. Dependence is a good thing. It keeps the home church praying and keeps the missionary on his toes. Experience has shown that missionaries who go to the field financially independent have some disadvantages. At times their sense of commitment to the team is reduced, they are tempted to be disdainful of leadership, and their ties with the home church tend to become weakened. I myself can name some outstanding exceptions to this generalization, but they do not disprove the rule. A bond of dependence with the church strengthens missionary work and ultimately is a blessing to the church itself.

How Much Missions Cost

How much does it cost to send a missionary and his family to the field these days? Like anything else, the cost is rising with current inflationary trends. It is rising even faster since the dollar has been devaluated on most foreign markets, decreasing the missionary's spending power there. One church recently had to add $17 thousand to its annual missionary budget, just to keep level with the official support increases of the mission boards. One thing this does *not* mean, however, is that missionaries are now getting rich!

Most missionaries are underpaid by homeland standards, but not all. One prominent denominational board calculates missionaries' salaries by determining the average salary of all U.S. ministers in the same denomination. Under this system, seminary graduates who go to the mission field invariably earn more than their friends who take a pastorate in a small church. The average total cost of sustaining a missionary family under this board is $20,000 per year.

This is a high figure. Most would be considerably lower. All boards, however, have to think in terms of such cost items as these:

1. *Salary.* Usually a family contains two missionaries, the husband and the wife, and they earn the same salary. Allowances are made for children in most missions. Traditionally, every missionary in the mission gets the same salary, regardless of responsibility or seniority, although some exceptions to this are being proposed. Salary for a missionary family of four or five might run around three hundred dollars per month, plus fringe benefits.

2. *Fringe benefits.* One hidden fringe benefit, which does not cost the home churches anything, is that missionaries pay no federal income tax since they qualify as "bona fide residents of foreign countries," even while on furlough. Some pay income tax in the country of residence, but this rarely is a burden. Housing is not included in the above salary figure, nor are children's education, medical insurance, social security tax, retirement, and sometimes modest travel allowances.

3. *Administrative costs.* As mentioned previously, mis-

sions like to keep the costs of homeland and field administration down somewhere below 20 percent of gross income, if at all possible. I have before me figures of two fine IFMA missions, one of which spends 19 percent on administration, and the other 8.9 percent. I happen to know, however, that the one that spends more uses a good bit of its administrative funds on research, planning, and seminars to educate their missionary personnel—an excellent investment of funds.

4. *Furlough costs.* In the past, most missionary terms consisted of five years on the field, and one year furlough. Modern transportation and changing life styles at home and abroad have now altered this pattern, however. Five years is now considered a longer term of service, and the trend is toward shorter terms and shorter furloughs. Naturally, this increases certain costs, but mission executives are generally agreed that the benefits more than make up for it. Nevertheless, the expenses of taking families back and forth up to halfway around the world must be built into realistic missionary budgets. Responsible missions include these costs in the total "support figure," rather than leave them as items for special fund-raising efforts when the date for furlough approaches.

5. *Field program.* Just getting missionaries to the field is not enough to develop a missionary program. Buildings, literature, vehicles, office equipment, guest homes, missionary children's schools, training institutions, social service programs, and scores of other items are needed for optimum missionary work. Missionaries cannot pay for these out of their salaries, so most missions have items built into the total "support figure" that include some of these costs. Over and above this, they present special projects one by one to their constituencies.

Put these all together, and you have the basis of a typical missionary support figure. This example is taken from a "faith mission" belonging to the IFMA, with a total in what would be considered the lower rates of support. A family of four in this mission needs to raise a monthly missionary support of:

Salary	$220.00
Transportation	30.00
Housing	40.00
Retirement	10.00
Medical insurance	29.00
Social security	16.00
Education	9.00
Furlough	66.00
Mission administration	63.00
Field program	53.00
Monthly family support	$536.00

This totals out to a yearly cost of $6,432. Few missions can hold a support level this low, but some do. In interdenominational missions, it is not unusual for the total to run around $1,000 per month for a missionary family of four. Even so, the yearly cost of $12,000 is considerably under the previously mentioned $20,000 of the denominational board.

Whatever the figure, it all ultimately comes from church members.

What Is the Church's Part?

How much is a church expected to do for missions?

Some churches have virtually no special interest in missions. As a matter of routine, they contribute to their denominational mission board program at the recommended level and let the board do the rest. Many of the members do not even know a real missionary personally, and their missionary I.Q. is practically zero. I have met Christian people like this and have found them usually very warm to missions. The fault generally is found, not in the pew but in the pulpit. A missionary-minded pastor can do wonders for an entire church if he develops a creative missionary program.

Some churches have decided to "tithe" their total income for missions. This is often above denominationally recommended amounts, but it is far from outstanding. The rule of thumb for churches that have been fired with a vision for a lost world in need of Christ is a minimum of 50 percent of the church budget for missions. They spend at least as much on reaching others for Christ as they spend on their own needs.

Boston's historic Park Street Congregational Church has become a model for a successful missionary program. With an assist from another of missions' superchurches, People's Church in Toronto (which annually gives over $500,000 to missions), they began their missionary effort in earnest in 1940. At that time church expenses were $31,000 and missionary giving totaled $17,000, which at 35 percent was not bad. But they reached the 50 percent mark in 1946, with over $50,000 for each item, hit a peak of 75 percent in 1957, and in 1972 they gave $364,593 to missions, a whopping 65 percent of the total budget. Little wonder that God has blessed the church in other ways, and that it is generally considered the Number One evangelical church in New England.

Few churches will duplicate Park Street's record, but all would do well to shoot for the 50 percent as a goal.

The Four Components of a Successful Program

Churches that have been successful in building strong and effective missionary programs have given special attention to four components:

1. The missionary chairman and his committee. I have spent my entire professional career in missions, but only recently has it begun to dawn on me how important missionary chairmen really are for the contemporary missionary enterprise. The light began to break when I realized that three fine Christian ladies, all of whom I know personally, together spend one million dollars a year on missions! This represents more financial muscle than any one of 65 percent of IFMA missions can muster.

These three ladies are the missionary chairmen of their respective churches.

To use a slightly worldly term, these women have incredible financial power! They themselves undoubtedly have never thought of their role as that of a powerhouse. But having been one myself, I know mission executives well enough to assert that they hold such missionary chairmen in great awe. If you add one hundred other missionary chairmen from comparable churches to these three, you have a relatively small group of people who, if they were so inclined, could virtually control U.S. missions. The Psalmist thanks the Lord for making him "as strong as a wild bull" (Ps. 92:10, *The Living Bible*). Missionary chairmen are as strong as bulls, but like most bulls, they have not discovered their own strength.

There is no merit in keeping them that way. The whole missionary cause would be boosted if missionary chairmen were encouraged. As I see it, they have four outstanding needs:

a. They need long terms. The missionary chairman should be the missiological expert of the church. In most cases, this role now goes by default to the pastor. Almost all pastors are interested in missions, but they are also interested in pastoral work. The very care of the flock in all but the smallest churches is enough to tax a man's full energy if he strives to do a first-class job. Most pastors would love to have someone else handle missions if they could only find someone dedicated enough to give the time and effort necessary to develop real expertise in the field.

This can only be accomplished on a long-term basis. Churches that change their missionary committees regularly and switch chairmen every year cannot hope for excellence. While the missionary chairmanship provides a fine opportunity for significant ministry for a part-time layman, as the budget grows it is not out of line to think in terms of a salaried person. It is scarcely possible to master the field of missions in less than five years. It might even take up to ten, depending on the amount of exposure the person has. Some should take it as a lifetime calling.

The committee members should be allowed to serve only on two conditions: (1) they will give at least three years to the responsibility, and (2) they will take their responsibility seriously enough to become well informed on missions through personal contact with missionaries and study of missionary literature.

b. They need travel funds. No one really has a grasp of missions unless he has been there. Long-term planning should get the missionary chairman, and perhaps the pastor as well, out to visit all of the church's missionaries on the field at least once a decade. These visits should be planned to include other action points of world missions. Funds for domestic travel should be available also, so that the chairman can meet from time to time with mission executives, visit other missionary conferences, and observe the missionary programs of other churches.

c. They need study opportunities. Workshops and short courses are available for missionaries, and many of these are just what missionary chairmen need. The Moody Bible Institute offers some outstanding missions study courses by correspondence. A missionary chairman ought to be receiving and reading the latest books on missions, Christian magazines, and journals with missions content. Sufficient funds for travel and study need to be built into the church missionary budget.

d. They need national recognition. Missionary chairmen aren't looking for ego trips, but the missionary cause would be enhanced if their position gained more dignity. When the Christian community realizes how important these chairmen are for the fulfillment of the Great Commission, missions will take a giant step forward. A friend of mine, for example, recently took an early retirement as vice-president of a bank in order to give the rest of his life to serving the Lord as a missionary chairman. If people only knew that such important opportunities for service were available, his number might increase one hundredfold. Something like an American Society of Church Missionary Chairmen needs to be formed so that these people can get to know each other, cross-fertilize their ideas, and build up an army of effective missionary workers in the home churches of the United States and Canada.

2. *The missionary conference.* Missions should be a constant part of the church program, but most churches have found it helpful to hold a special missionary conference at a certain time each year. There are many variations of format for missionary conferences, but the total impact should be to inform the congregation about what is happening in missions around the world, to update them on the works and workers supported by the church, and to challenge them for expanded service and giving.

The missionary conference has been the cornerstone of the development of Park Street Church's outstanding missionary program. It begins on a Friday in the Spring, and runs through the week to the following Sunday. Mission societies strive to send their best representatives to the conference, and it is considered a great privilege to be invited to speak. Each agency sets up attractive displays, designed to give the people an opportunity to see firsthand some of the things the missions are doing and to pick up the latest literature. Missionaries themselves are housed in the homes of church families so the people and the missionaries can get to know each other firsthand. This conference is so well planned that some people who do not live in the Boston area take a week's vacation, stay in a hotel, and benefit greatly from the conference.

The missionary conference is only the beginning of educating the church for missions. During the rest of the year, the missionary committee must maintain people's interest in missions. Attractive monthly inserts for church bulletins are available. Mission societies will send out their literature on request. The church library should be kept well supplied with books on missions. Something should be said about the missionaries in each Sunday's bulletin. The pastor should mention them regularly in congregational prayer. An attractive map of the world showing the location of the church's missionaries, and a well-arranged bulletin board help focus the vision of the "regions beyond."

3. *The missionary budget.* In order to maintain maximum challenge, the missionary committee should have the responsibility of designing the budget and of raising and spending the funds. Major items for a missionary budget will include:

a. Overhead. The costs of running the church missionary program are sometimes met from general funds and sometimes from funds designed from missions income. In any case, they should show in the total missions budget.

b. Contribution to the denominational program. This will be an item only where it applies. The amount of contribution depends on a multitude of variable factors, one of which is the degree to which the local church feels a part of the total program.

c. Direct support of missionaries. This is almost always the largest item in the budget. Some churches give small amounts to a great many missionaries, some give substantial amounts (up to full support) to a limited number of missionaries. While there are arguments on both sides, in my view it is not helpful to spread missionary funds too thin. Some are suggesting that churches strive for 60 percent to 100 percent support to missionaries who come from within their own ranks, and not drop below one hundred dollars per month of support for others. In that way, they will at least be assured that their own missionaries spend a reasonable part of their furlough in the local community, to the mutual benefit of the church and the missionary family alike.

Funds are needed, not only for the regular support of missionaries, but also for special needs. The printing and mailing of prayer letters, for example, is one item often overlooked by the church—only to become a great source of concern to the missionary. It is well to keep aside some contingency funds for emergency needs of heavily supported workers.

d. Project support. A portion of each year's budget should be available for the funding of projects that come to the attention of the missionary committee. Many of these projects will be related to the work that the church's own missionaries are doing, but some will not. Again, contingency funds are helpful in this category.

e. Research. For much too long, churches have glossed over the need for research. The businessmen on the missionary committee would not permit their corporations to operate without sufficient attention to research, but the principle has not yet carried over to missions in any significant way. The Fuller Seminary School of Missions, one of the nation's foremost centers of missionary research, suggests that 5 percent of every church's missionary budget be designated for missiological research. Such investments will pay off abundantly as new and creative approaches to missionary strategy are developed in the light of facts.

f. Education. The field of missions is one of the fastest-breaking areas of human knowledge. Missionaries who are on the field for three, four, or five years discover that they are out of it when they return. Many of them would love to study, but they cannot afford to. Forward-looking churches with creative missionary programs should make allowances for scholarships for their missionaries on furlough.

4. Raising the funds. To raise their missionary budget, churches usually adopt, with certain variations, one of two plans:

a. the church budget plan, or

b. the faith-promise system.

The church budget plan needs little explanation. Missions are presented to the church finance committee as another financial item, and the appeal is made to the congregation in one package.

More and more churches, however, are switching to the faith-promise system for missionary giving. In the annual missionary conference, each member is challenged to ask God to supply a certain amount of money through him from unanticipated sources. This is over and above the normal income. I could write another whole chapter around testimonies of how God has blessed this method and provided amazing amounts of money through the exercise of this kind of faith. In theory, the whole mission budget can be raised this way without touching the current church budget.

This actually happened in a church that we belonged to for some years. In 1970, when the missions budget of $7,200 was simply a part of the regular church budget, the whole church as well as the building fund went into the red. Finances became critical, so the missionary committee suggested switching over to the faith-promise system for missions. For that first year no goal was stated, but during 1970 all the $7,200 came in *apart from regular church giving*. The church itself went into the black and has been there ever since!

In 1971, they still were "ye of little faith" and set only $7,200 as the new goal. However, missionary giving went up to $8,500, and for the first time the committee had a surplus. In 1972, the goal was $11,640. This year it is $15,000. Doubling missionary giving in four years and adding to the general church budget at the same time constitute a good record in anyone's book. But for those who take the faith-promise system seriously, it seems to be the rule, not the exception.

When a church gets turned on for missions, the showers of blessing begin. If your church hasn't begun yet, you have a wonderful treat in store when you do.

And don't forget, they can't preach unless they're sent. You and your church have a key role in missions today.

For further reading:

Collins, Marjorie A. *Manual for Accepted Missionary Candidates.* South Pasadena, CA: William Carey Library, 1972.

"Questions and Answers on Faith-Promise Giving," by Russell D. Barnard (Palo Alto, CA: Overseas Crusades, Inc.).

The Fourth Dimension
of Missions: Strategy

Fourth dimensions are not always the most obvious. For many years philosophers and physicists alike described the world as three-dimensional: having height, breadth and depth. Then along came Einstein, and since then that elusive factor of time has been recognized as the fourth dimension.

Missions have a similar story. The first three dimensions are much more prominent in sermons, hymns, and textbooks than the fourth. The first dimension of missions is *height:* the relationship of man to God, reconciliation, the new birth. The second dimension is *depth:* personal holiness, spirituality, being "endued with power from on high" (Luke 24:49). The third dimension is *breadth:* witnessing, sharing Christ with those who are not yet Christians.

All three dimensions are essential to missions. But there is a fourth equally essential, namely *strategy.* Because strategy often tends toward the pragmatic, it appears to some as not being spiritual, and I have come up against some staunch resistance to developing it in any detail. An increasing number of missiologists, however, are recognizing the obvious fact that the use of the human mind is not always antagonistic to the Holy Spirit. After all, Jesus told us to love God with all our heart, with all our soul, and *with all our mind.* (See Matt. 22:37.) This is why I don't feel bad at all about using my mind as much as possible in developing missionary strategy. Of course, in order to avoid the dangers of carnality, the height and depth dimensions described above must be properly cared for as an indispensable precondition.

Strategy Is Not Optional

When you think of it, if you take Jesus and His lordship at all seriously, you are forced to develop a strategy of some kind. He demands that His stewards be found faithful (1 Cor. 4:1-2). Faithfulness, pure and simple, is doing what your Master tells you to do and accomplishing the goals He sets for you. The parable in Matthew 25:14-30, known as the Parable of the Talents, is a parable about stewards. Two of the three used good strategy and accomplished their master's goals (in that case, making wise investments of capital) and were called "good and *faithful* servants." One did not, and he was called "wicked and slothful." Anyone who does not take strategy seriously runs the risk of missing his reward at the judgment.

Strategy is the means agreed on to reach a certain goal. Missionary strategy is the way the body of Christ goes about obeying the Lord and accomplishing the objectives He lays down. I contend that every Christian every day uses strategy of some kind or other in the attempt to do God's will. I also contend that some strategies are demonstrably superior to others, and that we do poorly if we do not examine them all and choose the best.

The best strategy is, first of all, *biblical* because God's work must be done in God's way. Secondly, it is *efficient.* Since our personnel, money, and time are all limited, we need to make decisions sooner or later as to what priorities to assign in their use. We can't do everything we would like to do, so we must decide what to do and what to leave undone. We should make this decision on the basis of efficiency—do what will best accomplish God's objective. Third, strategy must be *relevant*. Missions is such a fast-moving field that strategy useful five years ago might well be obsolete today. It needs constant updating.

The Four Strategies of Missions

Modern missionary strategy is not simplistic. As a matter of fact, it is helpful to look, not at one strategy only, but at four strategies. I will list them here for convenience, then explain each one in detail:

Strategy I—the right goals;
Strategy II—the right place at the right time;
Strategy III—the right methods;
Strategy IV—the right people.

Strategy I—The Right Goals

Every one of Jesus' commands to His people contains a goal of some kind. There are hundreds of them in the New Testament, and faithful servants will want to obey them all in every way possible. But one command above all others contains the goal for missions, and against that goal we must evaluate all missionary strategy. This commandment is known as the "Great Commission," and it is found in Matthew, Mark, Luke, John, and Acts.

A proper understanding of the Great Commission will give us a clear picture of what God's goals for missions are. It goes without saying that God's goals are the *right goals*.

The place to start is Matthew 28:19-20, the most detailed and complete summary of the Great Commission. A proper interpretation of these verses will provide us with the key needed to understand the others in context. Here is what the text says: "Go therefore and make disciples of all nations, baptizing them in the name of the Father and of the Son and of the Holy Spirit, teaching them to observe all that I have commanded you. . . ."

Notice that the passage contains four action verbs: *go, make disciples, baptize,* and *teach.* In the original Greek only one of them is imperative, and three are participles. The imperative, *make disciples,* is the heart of the command. The participles *going, baptizing,* and *teaching,* are helping verbs.

Making disciples, then, is the end. It is the *right goal* of mission strategy. Going, baptizing, and teaching are means to be used toward accomplishing the end. They are also necessary components of missionary strategy, but they are not ends in themselves.

The other four appearances of the Great Commission do not expand on the right goal. They do add to the list of the means available to reach it. Mark 16:15,16 repeats baptizing, but adds preaching. Luke 24:47,48 repeats preaching, but adds witnessing. John 20:21 mentions sending. Acts 1:8, also written by Luke, repeats witnessing and adds the geographical aspect of Jerusalem, Judea, Samaria, and the uttermost part of the earth.

Now I will make a rather bold statement. *In my judgment, the greatest error in contemporary missionary strategy is the confusion of means and end in the understanding of the Great Commission.*

In other words, some missions and missionaries have set up their programs as though some of the means were ends in themselves. They have not adequately articulated what they are doing in terms of making disciples. Some, for example, have contented themselves with preaching the gospel whether or not their preaching makes disciples. Some have very meticulously counted "decisions," but they make no corresponding effort to count and report *disciples.* This is why some evangelistic reporting seems inflated. Just to know how many attended an evangelistic crusade or how many signed decision cards is helpful, but inadequate. The Lord of the Great Commission, in the final analysis, is interested in *disciples,* not simply *decisions.*

Don't forget, when we talk about right goals, we are talking about goals for the whole Body, not just for individuals. The doctrine of spiritual gifts teaches us that we all make different contributions. But as all members of the Body work together, the final result should be new disciples. Success or failure must be measured ultimately in those terms. One entire mission might concentrate on translating the Bible, for example. Bible translation is an essential function of the Body, for without the Word of God in the language of each people, they will not be able to hear the message of salvation. But proper strategy will coordinate this work with that of other members of the Body so that translated Bibles become, not just some more exotic contributions to the literature of mankind, but effective instruments for making disciples.

At this point be careful of the definition of *disciple.* If the right goal of missionary strategy is to make *disciples,* you absolutely have to know what Jesus was talking about if you plan to obey Him. You have to know how you can tell when you have made one. Nebulous ideas of what disciples are only serve to blur good strategy.

A person is not a disciple just because he has been born in a Christian country or, in many cases, even if he is a church member. We have already mentioned that decisions in themselves do not necessarily lead to disciples. Not everyone who prays to receive Jesus ends up a disciple. The basic meaning of disciple in the New Testament is equivalent to a true, born-again Christian. To go back to the terminology of chapter 1, everyone whose name is written in the *Lamb's Book of Life* is a disciple. Those who are not (including, unfortunately, many *World Christian Handbook* Christians) are not disciples in the Great Commission sense of the word.

In order to make a disciple, you need to go to the fourth world, to people not yet true Christians. Unsaved people are the raw material, so to speak, for fulfilling the Great Commission. The instant one becomes a "new creature in Christ" (2 Cor. 5:17), you have made a disciple.

Some have confused "making disciples" with "discipleship." *Making disciples* is the right goal of evangelism and missions according to the Great Commission. Once disciples are made, they then begin the lifetime road of *discipleship.* Helping people along the road is another important Christian ministry, an essential function of the body, but one step past the goal of the Great Commission. Even the participle "teaching" in the Great Commission itself does not refer to the details of the road of discipleship, as some might think. The thing taught in that verse is "to observe," not "all things I have commanded you." Part of becoming a disciple is to be disposed to obey Jesus. The details come later as the new disciple travels down the road of discipleship.

What does a disciple look like? How can you tell one when you see him? Acts 2 gives us a helpful indication. On the day of Pentecost three thousand disciples were made. The reason we know they were disciples and not just people who made "decisions" is that when Luke looked back in preparation for writing the book of Acts, they were "continuing steadfastly in the apostles' doctrine and fellowship and breaking of bread and prayers" (Acts 2:42). Outsiders can recognize disciples because "they have love one for another" (John 13:35).

If a mission society moves into a pagan village one year, and moves out three years later leaving a group of 250 people who declare that Christ is their Lord, who meet together regularly for worship, who read the Bible and pray—they have made 250 disciples and to that degree have fulfilled the Great Commission. These disciples might lack a great deal of polish. They might not act like Wheaton, Illinois, Christians. They might have a long way to go down the road of Christian discipleship, but nevertheless they are disciples. If the mission in question reports its results in such terms, it has properly understood Strategy I. It is aiming for the *right goals.*

Strategy II—The Right Place at the Right Time

Strategy II is best understood in agricultural terms. It comes out most clearly in some of Jesus' rural-oriented parables. As a farmer myself (my college degree is in dairy production!), I often jestingly suggest that being a farmer is more helpful in interpreting the parables than knowing Greek! The helpful aspect is that every farmer, by nature, has what I call the *vision of the fruit.*

No farmer works his fields for the fun of it—he works for the payoff, which is the fruit. A man buys a farm on the anticipation that it will produce fruit. He may enjoy mechanics, but he works on his machinery only because it will help him get the fruit. He sows his seed and cultivates his crops, not because he thinks it's fun to ride tractors, but because if he doesn't, there will be no fruit. "He that soweth and he that reapeth rejoice together" (John 4:36). Why? Because they gather fruit together.

Sound missionary strategy never loses the vision of the fruit. Strategy I teaches us that in missionary work this fruit is *disciples.* Keep this vision foremost in sowing, pruning and reaping.

1. The vision in sowing. The Parable of the Sower appears in Matthew, Mark and Luke. The briefest summary is in Luke 8:4-15. It tells of a farmer who sowed seeds on four different parts of his farm, but got fruit on only one. Anyone with the vision of the fruit will instantly ask, "Why?" Jesus' disciples undoubtedly asked the same thing when they first heard it.

According to Jesus' interpretation, the variable factor was not the sower, nor was it the seed (which is described

81

as the "word of God"), nor was it the method. It was the soil. No matter how good the seed is, any farmer knows it will not bear fruit on roadways, on rocky soil, or among thorns. In order to produce fruit, good seed must be sown in fertile soil.

The obvious lesson for missionary strategy is that the seed of the Word must be concentrated on fertile soil if fruit is to be expected. Some peoples of the world are receptive to the gospel while others are resistant. The world's soils must be tested. Concentrating, come what may, on rocky soil, whether or not any disciples are made, is foolish strategy. Farmers who have the vision of the fruit do not make that mistake too often, but some missiologists unfortunately do. This is the "right place" aspect of Strategy II.

2. The vision in pruning. The Parable of the Fig Tree in Luke 13:6-9 is seen as a threat by some missionaries. If they are guided by the vision of the fruit, however, it should not be.

The farmer who came along and saw a beautiful fig tree was forced to look a little deeper. The problem there was comparable to many mission fields. The fig tree had grown well, but there were no figs! Much missionary "work" has likewise developed to a high degree, but there is no fruit—no disciples. The farmer in the parable is a good strategist. When there is no fruit after much work and a prudent time lapse, he says cut it down—change your program. He operates on the basis of the vision of the fruit. His hired man does not share the vision because his income depends not so much on harvest as on a salary. His strategy is to continue the work as long as he can. He, like many missionaries, is program-centered, not goal-centered.

Missionaries who are comfortably settled into a certain "program" or "missionary work" would do well to examine what they are doing in terms of the vision of the fruit.

It is not easy to change a program, especially when you have been hoping against hope that in a year or so it will begin bearing fruit. But too often these years have stretched out into lifetimes. Missionaries who could have spent ten years making disciples spend the same ten years simply doing "missionary work" because they lack the courage to cut the barren fig tree down and change their program.

3. *The vision in reaping.* When Jesus talks to His disciples about reaping, for the first time He mentions the need for praying that the Lord of the harvest will "send forth laborers into his harvest" (Matt. 9:37–38). When the "laborers are few," the farmer runs the risk of losing some of the harvest. The Strategy II aspect in this case is the "right time." Laborers are not needed when the harvest is still green, nor are they needed when the harvest has passed. Timing is of utmost importance in any harvest.

Suppose, for example, that you owned an apple orchard. In Field A, a worker could harvest five bushels in an hour. In Field B, it would take him five hours to harvest just one bushel. In Field C, he couldn't harvest anything because the apples are all still green. If you had thirty workers today, where would you send them? I think I would send twenty-nine of them to Field A so as not to lose the fruit there. I would send the other one to do what he could in Field B and also to keep his eye on Field C. His job would be to let me know when those fields were ripe so I could redeploy the personnel.

Parallel situations arise time after time in missionary work. Some peoples are ready to be harvested today, some are not yet ready. These "unresponsive peoples" should not be neglected—someone should be there who is expert enough to tell when they are becoming ripe for the gospel. In one sense you need the very finest workers in the unresponsive fields. But no one who takes strategy seriously would advocate a massive labor force in green fields. Jesus wouldn't. He does not tell us to pray for more laborers to go to green fields or to fallow fields. The laborers are needed for the *ripe harvest* fields.

Right after Jesus says that in Matthew 9, He sends His own harvesters out in Matthew 10. There were three fields in those days: Jews, Gentiles, and Samaritans. Only the Jews were ripe at the time. Jesus specifically tells His disciples not to go to the Gentiles and Samaritans (Matt. 10:5) (the green fields), but to go to the Jews (Matt. 10:6). Later on both the Gentiles and the Samaritans ripened and bore much fruit, but not at that time.

Granted, it is not always the easiest thing to tell which soil is most fertile or just when a particular harvest is going to ripen in missionary work. Agricultural testing methods are much more advanced today than missiological testing methods. But missiologists are improving their methods all the time and making encouraging advances. A good deal is now known about testing peoples as to their degree of resistance or receptivity to the gospel. Up-to-date missions will take full advantage of such expertise, thus applying Strategy II—the right place at the right time.

Strategy III—The Right Methods

When there is much work and little or no fruit, something is wrong. Careful analysis will usually pinpoint the trouble as either working in unripe fields, or working in ripe fields, but using wrong methods. You can go into a perfectly ripe field of wheat and work your head off, but if you are using a cornpicker, you will get nothing. Potato diggers are useless in apple orchards.

Around the world there are peoples who would gladly receive the gospel and become Jesus' disciples, but missionaries among these people are not making disciples because they are using inappropriate methods.

The wrong language is one of the common methodological mistakes. In many cases on record the missionary thought that preaching in the trade language would be adequate for making disciples. Only when he switched to the local dialect, the language of the heart, however, did the fruit begin to come. If he had refused to change his methods, no amount of hard work would have done the job.

Mixing peoples has often proved to be another wrong method. For many years, for example, the Oregon Friends were reaping a great harvest among the Aymaras of Bolivia, while others working equally as hard were not. It was then discovered that the Friends insisted on keeping their churches purely Aymara, while others thought it well to mix mestizo believers with Aymaras. Missiologists call this *the principle of homogeneous unit churches*. Churches of one kind of people only are more effective in winning others of the same people. In Bolivia the method made the difference.

The list could be multiplied, but let's take a case closer to home. In 1959, D. James Kennedy was called to pastor the Coral Ridge Presbyterian Church in Florida. He began with a congregation of forty-five, but within a year it had dwindled to seventeen. He was so discouraged he considered leaving the ministry. A harvest field? Kennedy might well have concluded there was none at all.

But he changed his method. For one thing, he realized that if there was a harvest out there, it wouldn't come walking to him. He had to go out into the field and reap it. For another, he realized that the pastor can't do it all, and if effective evangelism is going to be done, the church has to begin functioning as a body. He then began a systematic program of house evangelism and trained a core of church members to help him. Strategy III worked. The harvest began to come in, and in ten years the church had grown from seventeen to twenty-five hundred!

Kennedy found a method that worked in his place at that particular time. Some fellow ministers have tried it with similar success, but others have tried it and have had scant results. Whenever a method is successful, the temptation arises to think it will work anywhere at any time. Strategy III is more complex than that, however. Every new situation requires a new evaluation and often new, tailor-made methods.

Methods must be selected on largely pragmatic factors, since the Bible does not pretend to give twentieth-century instructions. Therefore, it is good strategy not only to set measurable goals, but also to build in from the start of the effort instruments for measuring its success or failure. Only by doing this will it be possible to look back and know which methods God has blessed and which methods He has not blessed. One of the most curious facts in modern missions is that this simple procedure is so seldom carried out.

Strategy IV—The Right People

Some things God does by Himself; some things He does by using human beings.

It seems, for example, that the difference between fertile and barren soil is basically a matter of divine providence. The ripening of certain harvest fields at certain times can be attributed only to the sovereignty of God. "I have planted, Apollos watered," writes Paul, "but *God gave the increase*" (1 Cor. 3:6).

God brings the harvest to ripeness, but He does not harvest it. He uses Christian people to accomplish that task, and He is glorified when His people "bear much fruit" (John 15:8). He is particularly interested in "fruit that remains" (John 15:16). But how does this fruit come? The servant of God can only bear fruit if the branch abides in the vine. Jesus is the vine, and Christian people are the branches.

Strategy IV, then, stresses the right people. The right person is the person entirely filled with the Holy Spirit. He abides in Jesus. He is fully committed. He takes up his cross daily and follows his Master. Without Strategy IV, the first three strategies are dead letters. That is why Jesus insisted that His disciples not begin their missionary work until they were "endued with power from on high" (Luke 24:49).

Fourth dimensions might be elusive, but the sooner reliable strategy is properly appreciated and applied to missionary work, the faster the Kingdom of God will spread in the world.

For further reading:

Chandler, E. Russell. *The Kennedy Explosion.* Elgin, IL: David C. Cook Publishing Co., 1971.

Wagner, C. Peter. *Frontiers in Missionary Strategy.* Chicago: Moody Press, 1971.

Asking the Right Questions

In a field developing as rapidly as missions, at times it seems difficult for a person once removed from the inner circles to keep up on what is going on. Even some missionaries themselves, out on the front lines of the battle, exhausted by monsoons, mosquitoes, and malaria, find they have little energy or inclination to attempt to read the journals and relate to the intellectual currents swirling around the centers of missiology.

Even so, the average Christian wishes he were better informed about contemporary missionary issues. I have undertaken to select six more of what I consider the issues that will remain as focal points of missiological discussions in the years to come.

Redefining the "Indigenous Church"

Planting new churches is one of the chief responsibilities of missionaries. The word *baptize* in the Great Commission is commonly taken as a mandate to organize new-born disciples into local churches. Although this is a universally accepted principle, the resulting churches take on a wide variety of forms. This could be good or it could be bad. Much depends on whether the new churches are truly indigenous.

The concept of the indigenous church, as applied to those churches planted by missionaries all over the world, has traditionally included three aspects. The churches are to be: self-governing; self-supporting; self-propagating.

Until recently it has been assumed that when a church exhibits these three characteristics it is thereby "indigenous." Some missiologists, however, have now begun to question the adequacy of the three-self definition of the indigenous church. They do not think the current definition is *wrong,* they only contend that it is *incomplete.*

What is the problem? The problem is that all the three selfs could be in full operation, but the church could still be a foreign institution, considered by the nationals as a weird and irrelevant curiosity in their society.

A church like this is not truly indigenous, since the cultural aspect has not adequately been dealt with. A whole new breed of missionary anthropologists is making us all aware that a church planted on the mission field should so take on the characteristics of that culture that it is considered homegrown, or else it can never become a healthy, growing church.

There are some aspects of Christianity that must not yield to any culture at all. These are called transcultural elements. If people are in the habit of sacrificing human beings to the rain god, for example, this must stop. Drunkenness and debauchery have to go when the Holy Spirit takes over. Devil worship cannot continue. Adultery must fade in the white light of Christian ethics.

But watch out! Be sure you do not fall into the trap of defining adultery or other things the Bible condemns in terms that are bound to your own culture. Some missionaries who planted churches among polygamous peoples may have done just that. All agree that adultery means sexual relations outside of marriage. But the missionaries were not brought up in their culture to believe that a man could be *legally married* to more than one woman. The current opinion among missionary anthropologists is that many missions were hasty in insisting that a converted man leave all his wives but one before he could be baptized. This does not mean that they necessarily *approve* polygamy. They do suggest, however, that the transition could have been smoother, following more indigenous patterns. They contrast the phenomenal growth of the African independent churches to some slower-growing foreign churches to reinforce their point.

Don't forget, churches aren't ends in themselves. *Baptizing* is only one of the helping verbs, useful and necessary in accomplishing the Great Commission goal of making disciples, but not an end in itself. Some churches are useful in making disciples, but some are not. A major crippling factor in some churches is their lack of cultural relevance.

One of the outstanding examples might be the Christian church among Jewish people. A great deal of study is now being concentrated on discovering why conversions have been so infrequent among the Jews. Preliminary evidence indicates that the problem may lie in the area of cultural relevance. Many suspect that the hangup of the Jews is not nearly so much theological as it is cultural. Implicit in much previous missionary work among the Jews has been the unspoken requirement that if Jews want to be saved they must become Gentiles.

This is a reversal of the problem in the New Testament church. There the Judaizers insisted that Gentiles become Jews in order to be saved (Acts 15:1). Today some "Gentilizers" seem to have arisen. Is it really necessary for a Jew even to become a "Christian" in order to be saved? After all, the believers in the Jerusalem Church were not called *Christians,* but *disciples* or "followers of the Way" (Acts 9:2). Later on in Antioch, when Hellenists and Gentiles began coming into the church, the believers were first called *Christians* (Acts 11:26). The Jewish law certainly does not earn salvation, but could a person believe in Jesus as his Messiah and still continue to keep the law? Could a born-again believer worship on Saturday and keep a kosher kitchen?

These are the questions being raised by those anxious to see the door to the salvation of Israel opened. When they get the answers and discover what a church truly indigenous to the Jewish culture really looks like, they might well have the key.

The Syndrome of Church Development

It is so easy for a good missionary to get sidetracked! In fact it can even happen to a whole mission, and it has.

One of the most common ways of getting sidetracked is to fall into what I like to call the *syndrome of church development.* If I were to make a catalog of missionary maladies, I would put this one high on the list. It cripples more missionaries than hepatitis, dysentery, and malaria put together.

When a missionary first goes to what we have called the *fourth world* to preach the gospel and bring men and women to Christ, there is no danger of the syndrome of church development, mainly because there is no church yet. The missionary has his priorities right: he concentrates on those people who do not yet know Christ. But as soon as some are baptized, and as soon as a church is organized, he'd better watch out. He can easily get so fascinated by the new little church that he forgets why he went to the mission field in the first place.

The little church has so many needs. Although the missionary knows he shouldn't be paternalistic, he has a difficult time suppressing his desire to shower an abundance of love and care on the newborn babes. The new believers are hungry for spiritual things; they need counseling to straighten out some of life's tangled problems; they want Bible teaching. Leaders need to be trained; literature must be produced in the vernacular; a church building is waiting to be constructed; someone who is trustworthy should be instructed to handle church finances. The believers need to be warned of heresy, taught the Lord's prayer and the Apostles' Creed, and instructed in witnessing. A Sunday School is needed. They have to learn the hymns, and someone needs to accompany congregational singing with an accordion; they are poor and need financial help; the farmers could increase production with a little instruction; when they get sick someone has to take them to the doctor. The items in this list could easily be doubled or tripled. Even in a small church, they add up to much more than one missionary can ever hope to do.

It happens so often, though. The missionary begins to get deeply involved in church affairs. He knows he should trust the Holy Spirit to fill the new believers, to give them spiritual gifts, to lead them into all truth (see John 14:26), but he feels they need a little boost from him. So far, so good. New believers do need some attention. Only irresponsible evangelists would bring people to Christ and then abandon them. But taking care of new churches can easily become habit-forming. A small dose of fatherly care is good, but when it becomes compulsive paternalism, when the missionary finds himself addicted, he has tumbled into the syndrome of church development.

Few things can quench missionary effectiveness as thoroughly as the syndrome of church development. The goal of good missionary strategy is to make disciples. But, as we have seen, disciples cannot be made in the *church*—they are made only in the *world*. Every missionary who lets himself get pulled out of the world and involved in developing the church is reducing the total effectiveness of his missionary society in fulfilling the Great Commission. This has become so much the pattern in some missionary societies that they no longer even call missionaries by that name. They call them "fraternal workers!"

Take a close look at your favorite mission. List in parallel columns the names of the workers who are engaged in winning people to Christ and planting new churches as over against those who are developing the church. If even 25 percent are in the first column, the mission can be considered reasonably evangelistic. Most missions will be so overbalanced in the second column that you will immediately see they have fallen into the syndrome of church development.

This not only reduces effectiveness in making disciples, but, ironically, it hinders church development itself. There is almost an inverse proportion between paternalism and church quality. The more paternalism, the worse the church. This is one of the reasons why on many mission fields the so-called "indigenous movements," meaning the churches that have developed with little or no foreign missionary influence are growing much faster than the nonindigenous ones. Thus, it is a painful fact that well-meaning missionaries who have not been adequately warned of the dangers of the syndrome of church development sometimes end up by doing more harm than good on the mission field!

Of course, I do not mean that no missionaries at all need to get involved in church-development ministries. That would be ridiculous. I am just saying that if we have sinned at all and thrown our priorities out of balance, we have usually done so in that direction. World wide, churches that suffer usually complain of too much, not too little, paternalism. That's one reason why you so often hear the cry, "Missionary, go home."

Diagnostic Research in Evangelism

A milestone in contemporary missiology was the publication, in 1973, of Vergil Gerber's *Manual for Evangelism/Church Growth,* not only in English but also in several other languages. Widespread and conscientious use of this little book and its principles on every mission field will mean significant progress in the fulfillment of the Great Commission.

Gerber's Section III is entitled, "Aids for Diagnostic Research." Such step-by-step, do-it-yourself instructions for evaluating the effectiveness of evangelistic programs have been long overdue. Through diagnostic research, your physician can tell whether an organ of your body is properly fulfilling its bodily function. It is healthy if it is accomplishing its goal.

By the same token an evangelistic program, whether this involves only a local church or an entire missionary society, can be evaluated by diagnostic research. The goal, according to Strategy I in the preceding chapter, is to *make disciples.* The reason I spent so much time stressing how you could tell when you had made a disciple was precisely so that the concept would be useful in diagnostic research. Disciples are countable; they provide hard data for diagnosing the health of your evangelistic program.

In a way I hate to say it, but it is sadly true that the mission fields of the world are overloaded with evangelistic programs that are not functioning properly. Sadder yet, many people deeply involved in them don't even realize the fact. The symptoms of the disease are effectively masked by a great amount of activity, long hours of work, flamboyant advertising, high-pressure spiritual exercises for the believers, large expenditures of funds, and all other things that add up to a superevangelistic program. The program *should* bring multitudes of unsaved people to Christ, but it *doesn't!*

In many of these programs, believe it or not, the results are not even tested. It is just *assumed* that all the hard work has paid off. Sometimes the verse, "My word . . . shall not return unto me void," (Isa. 55:11) is quoted as a device to avoid the responsibility of checking results against investments.

95

Almost accidentally, I began to do diagnostic research on one of our massive evangelistic programs in Bolivia some years ago. Along with all the others involved, I had simply assumed that large numbers of disciples had been made as a result. Had we not invested over a year of time? Were not thousands of church members trained in personal evangelism? Did not multitudes of believers meet weekly in cells for earnest prayer? Were not radio and literature used extensively? Did not the visitation, the congresses, and the campaigns bring a large percentage of Bolivia's population under the hearing of the gospel? Were we not exhausted when it was all through? Did we not record over twenty thousand decisions for Christ?

The answer to all these questions was yes. But we were foolish enough to believe that we also had effectively accomplished the goals of Strategy I—*making disciples.* When we undertook diagnostic research some years later, however, we discovered that the growth rate of the major churches involved had actually declined rather than increased! Subsequent research in other countries has shown that Bolivia was not an exception to the rule. It was bad news, just as it is when your doctor's diagnostic research shows that you need an operation. But in spite of the pain, you're glad that he discovered the disease now rather than letting it kill you.

Good diagnostic research can still save many of our evangelistic programs, if it is carried out with courage and skill. Theological seminaries need to include such research in their curricula. If only the current fad of holding nation-wide, regional, and even world congresses on evangelism could be harnessed to teach diagnostic skills to church leaders across the board, the cause of evangelism and missions would be advanced in a spectacular way.

Short-Term Missionary Service

A generation ago, almost everyone who volunteered for

missionary service assumed that he would give a lifetime to the work. Nowadays, however, an increasing number of young people hesitate to make a hasty commitment for life. The new generation has been accused of being less spiritual. I doubt that. Perhaps they are simply wiser and more cautious than their fathers. Besides, they have some new options open to them.

I have not been able to discover exactly how many Americans are currently out on short-term missionary assignments. My guess would be that, counting those who go for the summer only, the figure would be somewhere over five thousand. The average term of service is one year. But it can be as much as five years and as little as two or three months, depending on the circumstances.

I like to classify short term missionaries as follows:

1. *Skilled workers.* Men and women with particular skills are accepted by a mission society for a stated task. They know their job description before they leave for the field, and they also know how long they expect to serve.

Short-term service provides a magnificent opportunity for young people, or older ones for that matter, to test their missionary gift. One couple came to our missionary children's school for a two-year term, sent by Short Terms Abroad of Downer's Grove, Illinois. After four months they decided they had the missionary gift and applied for full career membership in the mission. Another couple was sent to the school for one year by their own church missionary committee. Before the year was over, they discovered that they did *not* have the missionary gift, although they had made a good contribution to the school. In my opinion, the test was successful in both cases. The Lord spoke to the latter couple as clearly as to the former. Now they are happily settled in the U.S.A., active in their church, better Christians because of their year's experience on the mission field, and free of any nagging guilt feelings that they might have had if they had not tested their gifts.

The one drawback in the case of short-term skilled workers is that they cannot take time for a full course in language school. But there is much they can do in English. Hostesses for guest homes, farm managers, airplane pilots, school teachers, dentists, houseparents, radio technicians, typists, accountants, cooks, and scores of other jobs are open to qualified short-term workers who know only one language.

2. Interns. Interns are workers who are building a year of foreign service into their training programs. Typically, an intern will take off one year from Bible school or seminary to become involved in missionary work. Often he will receive some academic credit for his involvement.

Since the year is an integral part of training, the program for interns is often developed not so much according to what the intern will contribute to the mission's work as to what the mission can contribute to the intern's training. It often works both ways, however.

3. Summer students. More and more Christian young people are spending their summers on the mission field. Some are sent by mission boards, some by their schools, some by their churches, and some just go to visit friends and relatives there.

Some missions design their programs in order to put the summer students to work. They may distribute tracts, hack a dugout canoe, type a book manuscript, or paint a campground. I have some reservations about this approach, however. While summer students undoubtedly should be assigned some unskilled labor during their time on the field, this should not be their only objective. In addition to accomplishing something for the mission, they should have at least an equal opportunity for a full and realistic exposure to as many aspects of missionary life as possible. They should gain as complete an orientation to native life as they can in the short time available, and they should take home a positive impression of missionary work.

Above all, they should be tuned in to the need for testing to see whether they have the missionary gift. Even a brief exposure like this will be sufficient for many to reach a conclusion.

Theological Education by Extension

Although it is impossible to do justice to the vast subject of theological education by extension in a couple of pages, this would not be an up-to-date picture of missions without it. TEE, as it is called for short, started in Guatemala in 1962 and since then has spread not only around Latin America but throughout the world. Without doubt, it is now one of the most significant aspects of modern missions, and TEE will continue to provide an outstanding challenge for missionary teachers for a decade or two to come. Here is a wide-open field for missionary candidates with the gift of teaching.

The need for rethinking theological education on the mission field came when some diagnostic research was done over a decade ago. It was discovered that present-day Bible schools and seminaries were not able to train the quantity of pastors needed in already existing churches; rapid church growth was pushing the situation from bad to worse, and traditional residence programs were often not producing the quality of leaders needed for the churches.

Once the traditional program of residence instruction was found inadequate, a new one was engineered. It was decided to take the seminary out to the students rather than make the students come to the seminary. Professors would visit their students in their villages once a week. By doing this, many church leaders with the gifts of the Spirit needed for ministry could get seminary training that was not available to them previously. Most of these men were older leaders whose jobs and families would not permit them to take off two or three years for residence training.

In Latin America alone, over ten thousand church leaders are now taking seminary training without leaving their villages or their churches. TEE is much more than a correspondence course, since it requires frequent face-to-face contact between students and instructors. It has even been discovered that in many instances the educational quality of TEE, which uses self-instructional materials and creative seminar sessions, has been superior to a more traditional training, which extracts the student from his own environment.

TEE may become one of the few major innovations in the American church to have originated on the mission field. Some prominent seminaries in our country are now instituting TEE programs, and undoubtedly the trend will increase. When the influence comes from the mission field back to the sending country, a notable switch has taken place.

The next chapter will show how something similar may be happening on an even broader scale.

For further reading:

Gerber, Vergil. *A Manual for Evangelism/Church Growth.* South Pasadena, CA: William Carey Library, 1973.

Covell, Ralph R. and Wagner, C. Peter. *An Extension Seminary Primer.* South Pasadena, CA: William Carey Library, 1971.

Full Circle:
Third World Missions

God never intended missions to stop, at least until this age is over and Jesus returns.

That's why all the talk about the age of missions being over and about missionaries being no longer needed or wanted is nonsense. More missionaries than ever before should be moving out to the fields of the world if Christians are going to follow God's game plan.

One of the problems is that we have tended to see missions as a straight line rather than as a circle. We have foolishly supposed that missions have a starting point and an ending point and that the job can be completed in a given period of time. If you consider Christ's second coming as the end point, all right. But we can't live as though He's coming tomorrow, although it may well be that He will. In the meantime, God expects us to live and work as though He were *not* coming. That means we need to continue and even increase our missionary efforts. We need to view Christian missions as a continuous cycle, turning around and around with no foreseeable end in sight.

What Color Are Missionaries' Feet?

Several times in this book we have quoted the missionary passage in Romans 10. We have stressed the evangelistic mandate to preach the gospel, and we have stressed the need to send missionaries to do it. As this happens, we can then say with God: "How beautiful are the feet of those who preach the Gospel of peace with God and bring glad tidings of good things" (Rom. 10:15).

Now when you think of all those missionary feet going out, what color feet do you see?

Probably white!

No argument. It is a fact of life that the bulk of the missionary work up to now has been done by white Westerners. When you think of missionaries, you think of Americans or Englishmen or Canadians or Europeans or Australians or New Zealanders. The image is only natural because these people come from the countries where Christianity has been most deeply rooted throughout the centuries.

But no longer! The largest Presbyterian church in the world, for example, is not in Scotland or in the U.S.A., but in Seoul, Korea. The Christian and Missionary Alliance Church has more members in Indonesia than in the U.S.A. Statistics show that by the turn of the century, a full 60 percent of the world's Christians will be found in the Third World: Asia, Africa, and Latin America. Very soon Christianity will no longer be a white man's religion. Hallelujah! This means that the Christian missionary enterprise has been much more successful than William Carey or David Livingstone or Robert Morrison could have imagined in their fondest dreams.

One of the results of this new fact of world Christianity is that the feet of all those missionaries marching out with the message of Jesus Christ are going to change color. Not that there will be fewer white feet—heaven forbid! But these white feet will be joined by a vastly increasing number

102

of brown, black, red and yellow feet. Even now the churches of the Third World are beginning to send out their own missionaries to win people to Christ and plant churches.

Missions 360 Degrees

This had to happen because missions are not a straight line: Westerners to the Third World—period. Missions are a circle, and God delights in 360-degree missions.

Here are the quadrants in the full circle of missionary activity:

90°—the mission sends out missionaries to a certain people to preach the gospel, win men and women to Christ, and plant Christian churches.

180°—the seed of the Word bears fruit, people are saved, and a new church is planted. The new church is still under mission supervision and care.

270°—the church gains its autonomy, it begins to take care of its own affairs, and the mission either stays under a "partnership" agreement or moves elsewhere. Most of our mission programs today have been 270-degree programs. Some missions have even pulled out of the field when they turned the church over to the nationals, arguing that they had "worked themselves out of a job." This is simply another, less obvious, variation of the syndrome of church development that was described in the last chapter. Notice the fallacy: the decision as to the future direction of the mission is taken on the basis of the *church* that is already there instead of on the basis of the *challenge* to win thousands of people in the community who do not yet know Jesus personally. The missionary doesn't work himself out of a job until every conceivable winnable person is won to Christ and continuing faithfully in the apostles' doctrine, in fellowship, in breaking of bread, and in prayers.

360°—missions go full circle when the new church that is planted by the first mission gives birth to a mission of its own. The old concept of a self-propagating church too often referred to the 270-degree position—the church would be capable of keeping itself alive. But the 360-degree position insists that this church not only keep itself going, but also generate other churches in other cultures. In other words a 360-degree church is a missionary-minded church.

Generally speaking, our missionary work over the past 150 years has been 270-degree work. We have planted many indigenous *churches,* but we have not adequately stressed planting indigenous *missions.* A top Chinese Christian leader once said, "Most of my missionary friends confess that they have never preached a single sermon on missions to the young churches." I think he is right. While on furlough, missionaries preach great sermons to fire up their friends for missions, then they file the sermons when they go back to the field. Missionaries themselves unconsciously propagate the idea that missions is a Western task. The feet are all white!

That splendid New Testament church of Antioch gives us a biblical model for 360-degree missions. Here's how it happened:

90°—"Men of Cyprus and Cyrene, when they were come to Antioch, spoke unto the Greeks, preaching the Lord Jesus" (Acts 11:20). The missionaries arrived and began preaching their message.

180°—"A great number believed and turned to the Lord" (Acts 11:21). A new, national church had started, but the mission continued to help—first by sending Barnabas from Jerusalem (see Acts 11:22), and then by bringing Paul over from Tarsus (Acts 11:25).

270°—"For a whole year they assembled themselves with the church and taught many people. And the disciples were called Christians in Antioch" (Acts 11:26). By that time the church was no longer dependent on the mission. They even gave offerings to the mother church (Acts 11:27–30).

360°—"As they ministered to the Lord and fasted, the Holy Spirit said, Separate me Barnabas and Saul for the work to which I have called them" (Acts 13:2). So the church became a sending church, and two of history's greatest missionaries went out to plant new churches (Acts 13:3–4).

The Green Lake Consultation

In 1971, a major consultation of IFMA and EFMA mission executives was called in order to discuss relationships between missions and national churches. Four hundred top leaders met in Green Lake, Wisconsin, for a week, wrestling with the problems that faced them all. While there, it occurred to the delegates that the sending churches needed to be included in the study, but the conference even so turned out to be at only the 270-degree position. The problem was that *sending* churches were still synonomous with *Western* churches. The feet were still all white.

Nevertheless, Green Lake was a milestone because there the new trend began. The change did not come in the program itself; it came through conversation in the corridors as individuals realized that there was a gap between 270-degree missions and 360-degree missions. A major catalyst was a Korean team, David Cho and Samuel Kim, an executive and a missionary of the Korea International Mission, a real, live 360-degree mission. They should have had a prominent part on the program, but they didn't because the conference planning was bogged down at the 270-degree quadrant.

I do not mean to imply that the executives at Green Lake were ignorant of what was occurring in parts of the world such as Korea. Most were aware that some Third World churches were sending missionaries out. At that time the matter simply was not considered that *important* for a North American missionary consultation.

The ideas generated in the corridors first surfaced in a significant way in the book that was written after Green

Lake by thirteen of the participants *(Church/Mission Tensions Today,* C. Peter Wagner, ed.). Three of the chapters were particularly relevant to what was then being called *Third World Missions.* Grady Mangham of the Christian and Missionary Alliance wrote a chapter on the outstanding progress that his mission had made in helping Asian churches to go 360 degrees. Ian Hay of the Sudan Interior Mission described how the West African churches established a mission board and sent out one hundred missionary couples. And Fuller Seminary's Ralph Winter dealt with the missiological aspects in a chapter called "Planting Younger Missions."

Once this happened, it seemed that interest in 360-degree missions perked up all over the place. More information was needed. Exactly what was happening out there in the Third World? In order to answer these questions, a small research team was organized at the Fuller School of Missions; the team was composed of James Wong, Edward Pentecost, and Peter Larson. I had the privilege of coaching them. Several months of intensive research by the team led to the publication of their book *Missions From the Third World*—the first worldwide account of what is being done.

Defining the Third World

Before sharing some of the results, let's pause to define terms. What, exactly, do we mean by *Third World Missions?*

Back in Chapter One, we briefly discussed the term *Third World,* and concluded that it refers generally to Asia, Africa, and Latin America. It might be helpful at this stage to refine the definition somewhat. We need to know what part of the world we are including and what part we are excluding. Some countries are easy to place. For example the United States, Russia, and Germany are clearly not Third World. Burundi, Cambodia, and Bangla Desh clearly are. What is the criterion?

It cannot be strictly *economic.* We cannot say that only the underdeveloped countries are Third World. That would exclude countries such as Japan.

It cannot be strictly *cultural.* If only non-Western countries are Third World, most of the nations in Latin America, which consider themselves Western nations, would be excluded.

It cannot be strictly *political.* If you say that Third World nations are those nonaligned to the Communist or to the capitalist worlds, you would leave China out, for example.

It cannot be strictly *geographical.* There are Third World peoples on all continents. As a matter of fact, right here in the U.S.A. we have Third World peoples, such as many of our blacks, Spanish-Americans, Indians, and Orientals.

As I see it, the definition of *Third World* is best considered as *psychological.* The mentality of a people classifies them in the Third World. This mentality means that a certain people feel themselves independent to some significant degree of the two great Western power blocks, although of course hardly anyone in today's shrinking world can claim absolute independence. Granted, this psychological definition is not cut and dried enough to be reduced to a mathematical formula, but experience has shown that it is useful. By it South African blacks, East Indians, Mainland Chinese, Colombians, and many others like them feel that they have certain important things in common.

Defining Missions

One thing that is happening among Third World peoples is that they are beginning to send out missionaries to propagate the Christian faith. What do we mean by *missionaries* in this context? Throughout this book we have been stressing that missionaries are those sent to spread the gospel across cultural boundaries. This is still the basic definition, but there is one category of missionary that it would not include—those missionaries, for example, who are sent by the Japanese church to plant churches among Japanese colonists in Brazil. They go a long way geographically, but do not cross cultures.

In order to be specific about what is included in Third World Missions and what is not, the Fuller Seminary research team has devised a classification system, using M and G as the symbols.

M stands for missions, and is divided into three subcategories as follows:

1. *Missions-one (M_1)*. These are missionaries who go to plant churches in their same culture, like "Jerusalem and Judea" of Acts 1:8. The Japanese mentioned above who is a missionary to his own people in Brazil would fit in here.

2. *Missions-two (M_2)*. These missionaries go to another culture, but the difference between the two is not a radical difference. In Acts 1:8, "Samaria" would be the example. An equivalent today would be an Italian missionary working in Caracas, Venezuela.

3. *Missions-three (M_3)*. M_3 missionaries go to a radically different culture or to the "uttermost parts of the earth" as in Acts 1:8. A Korean missionary serving in Ghana would be an example today.

How far these people go is the other important dimension. Those who leave their homeland's borders encounter a particular set of problems that they would not encounter if they stayed home. G, then, stands for geography, and is divided into two subcategories:

1. *Geography-one (G_1)*. The worker ministers in his own homeland. This would include a missionary from Illinois to the Navajos in Arizona. We used to call these *home missions*.

2. *Geography-two (G_2)*. The worker has to leave his own country in order to get to the place where he is sent. Most missionaries are G_2 missionaries.

There are six possible combinations of these factors, as

is seen in the following chart. Of them, only those workers who stay in their own country and minister to those of their own culture are excluded from the category of Third World Missions.

Classification of Third World Missions

	G_1	G_2
M_1	Not Included	Yes
M_2	Yes	Yes
M_3	Yes	Yes

Extensive research has shown that most of the 2 billion plus people in the world who do not yet know Jesus Christ will be won only by M_2 and M_3 missionaries. Because of our 270-degree mentality, however, we have stressed mostly M_1 in our churches overseas. The great Berlin World Congress on Evangelism, held in 1966, was almost exclusively M_1. Little or no stress was given to M_2 or M_3 evangelism. Little wonder that the regional and national successors of Berlin stressed M_1 as well. This has been a very serious oversight.

With the recent awareness of these facts, efforts have been made to bring the Lausanne Congress projected by Billy Graham for 1974 around to a 360-degree position. Some suggested that it be called a "Congress on World Evangelism and Missions," but this did not go through. Instead it will be a "Congress on World Evangelization," and it is hoped that Third World missions will be prominent on the program. The appointment of a missionary, Donald Hoke, as the general coordinator is a favorable sign.

Even though it is admittedly incomplete, Wong, Pentecost, and Larson's report lists 210 sending agencies, and calculates that they are sending out over three thousand missionaries. These missionaries' feet are brown, red, black, and yellow!

The leading countries, according to this preliminary data are:

1. Nigeria   820 missionaries
2. India   598 missionaries
3. Brazil   595 missionaries
4. U.S.A. (Third World) 448 missionaries
5. Philippines   170 missionaries
6. Japan   137 missionaries
7. South Africa   84 missionaries
8. Mexico   69 missionaries
9. Oceania   61 missionaries
10. Korea   38 missionaries

New Names in Mission History

All this is not so new as most people think. A few of our well-known Western missions have been working on this for some time, but they are all too few. The Christian and Missionary Alliance, the Sudan Interior Mission, the Southern Baptists, and the Overseas Missionary Fellowship are four that have made substantial contributions. Others have much to learn from them. But Third World missions go back farther than that.

In the 1820s, for example, missionaries like Josua Mateinaniu were hopping from one island to another in the Pacific. This is one reason why Oceania is almost entirely Christian today. In the 1830s, some Jamaicans, led by Joseph Merrick, pioneered the missionary movement to the Cameroons. By 1884, Methodist missionaries were going out from India to Malaysia. In 1907, the Korean Presbyterians began sending missionaries, among the first being Kee Pung Lee. One of history's most effective missionary societies, called the Melanesian Brotherhood, was organized in the 1920's in Oceania. Having taken vows of poverty, celibacy, and obedience, Ini Kopuria and other great heroes of the faith went out, barefoot and bareheaded, to propagate the gospel.

Names like Hudson Taylor and David Brainerd and Robert Moffat are well known in missionary history. But Josua Mateinaniu, Joseph Merrick, Kee Pung Lee, and Ini Kopuria should take a place with them when the real, worldwide history of missions is written. Most of the protagonists of our missionary biographies still have white feet.

Missions at Bargain Prices

Third World missions are able to do some things that seem unreal to traditional Western missions. You will remember, for example, that in chapter 5 we mentioned that it costs from sixty-five hundred dollars to twenty thousand dollars per year to maintain a U.S. missionary family on the field. Well, the Evangelical Missionary Society of Nigeria, an agency related to the Evangelical Churches of West Africa, is sending out around one hundred missionary couples on a total yearly budget of twenty thousand dollars for the whole mission! If, as I contend, good missionary strategy needs to be efficient, there is some efficiency factor built in here that others of us can learn from.

How do they do it?

I myself would like to know much more about how they do it. But I have some clues from a series of mimeographed reports I have recently received from survey teams led by the E.M.S. Secretary, Panya Baba. The reports describe new areas, attempt to locate the most responsive peoples, make recommendations for church planting, suggest the number of missionaries needed, and then a section follows: "How the Evangelist Might Make a Living." This report assumes that the missionaries will so identify with the people that they will make their own living right where they minister. Among the possible occupations are poultry raising, vegetable gardening, growing fruit trees, tailoring, and merchandising. A report like that wouldn't recruit many white-footed missionaries, but apparently large numbers of black-footed missionaries are accepting the challenge.

In 1958, a group of concerned Indian Christians from the Church of South India held a prayer meeting at Kovilpatty. At that time they formed the Friends Missionary Prayer Band. They worked with M_1-G_1 evangelism for some time, but in 1971, God gave them a vision for North India, an M_2 and M_3 challenge. They chose eleven states of North India and promised God that they would send at least two missionaries to each district of those states in ten years. It added up to 220 districts, so they were committed for 440 missionaries. Let's admit it: such faith would stagger many U.S. missionary executives!

They reasoned that each prayer group could support one missionary. You have to commit your funds to missionary support before you can even join one of these groups. All they would need, they calculated, were 440 prayer groups to reach their goal!

In less than two years, believe it or not, thirty full-time workers have already been sent out. Their income went up from four thousand rupees in 1966 to forty-eight thousand rupees in 1971. They fully expect to have their 440 missionaries on the field by 1981!

Other countries are moving as well. In Japan, for example, eleven missionary sending agencies have formed an organization called Japan Overseas Missions Association, with a permanent office in Tokyo run by Andrew Furuyama. A similar number of societies in Korea have banded together in what they call the Korean Foreign Missions Association. David Cho is their first Executive

Director. These organizations parallel the IFMA and EFMA here in the USA. Continentwide consultations are being projected to advance Third World missions.

With organizations like the Evangelical Missionary Society of Nigeria and the Friends Missionary Prayer Band of India, missions are coming full circle. Let me repeat—this does not mean that we need *fewer* white-footed missionaries, we need *more*. But they will no longer be alone as the gospel continues to circle the globe with ever-increasing power. Every black, brown, red, and yellow foot that joins the army of God's soldiers will help hasten that glorious day when those from every tongue, tribe, and nation will proclaim Jesus as Lord.

For further reading:

Wong, James; Larson, Peter and Pentecost, Edward. *Missions from the Third World.* Singapore, Church Growth Study Center, 1973. Available in the U.S.A. from William Carey Library, 533 Hermosa Street, South Pasadena, CA 91030.

Wagner, C. Peter, ed. *Church/Mission Tensions Today.* Chicago: Moody Press, 1972.

Launch Out
into the Deep

CHAPTER 9

One day Jesus taught His disciples a lesson about missions they never forgot.

Those disciples were fishermen, so He taught them something about fishing. It's all recorded in Luke 5:4-10.

Jesus related his teaching to the fishermen's own goal: a great catch of fish (v. 4). This goal made sense to the disciples because they were *professionals*. All fishermen aren't pros, of course. Some people go fishing just for the enjoyment of being out in the fresh air and getting away from the normal routine of life for a while. Amateur fishermen get satisfaction from fishing whether they catch anything or not. They *prefer* to catch something, they even make up fantasies when they don't, but they nevertheless go back again and again when they don't. They enjoy the fishing as much as the fish.

Not professionals! They have to take fishing more seriously than that because their living depends on it.

Jesus was talking to *professional* fishermen, but He made it clear that He was not really talking about fish. He said, "From henceforth thou shalt catch *men*" (v. 10). This reinforces the Strategy I goal of the Great Commission—to make disciples. Jesus wanted His disciples to take His work at least as seriously as they took their fishing. He wants

115

a great multitude of disciples, and He is not satisfied with less.

There is much amateur thinking in missions today. Amateur thinking is satisfied with fishing without catching. I have heard expressed ideas such as these:

• God wants us to fish strenuously for men. He is pleased if we put in long hours, use creative fishing techniques, keep our equipment up to date, and read the latest angling literature, but He is not particularly concerned whether we catch anything or not.

• God does not expect us to keep records of how many fish we catch. As long as we keep working hard, He will take responsibility for the results and for keeping track of how well we are doing. We will only know if we have caught anything when we get to heaven.

• A smaller catch of fish is usually a higher *quality* than a great multitude, and furthermore they're much easier to keep in the boat. We prefer quality to quantity.

The professional fishermen in Luke's story knew better than that, but nevertheless they had fished all night and caught nothing. They were tired and discouraged. Their program had failed. Like many missionaries today, they had the resources, they had the experience, and they worked hard. But they had been fishing without catching.

Then Jesus came along and said, "Launch out into the deep" (v. 4). I can imagine how this advice from a *carpenter* struck these exhausted *fishermen* when they first heard it. They were disappointed with their evening's performance, but they were tired, they wanted something to eat, and they wanted to get some sleep. Their nets were already washed, and they were reconciled to defeat.

But although Jesus was no fisherman. He was *Lord.* So they argued a little, but they changed their plans and obeyed Him. What they didn't know at the time was that Jesus, with divine wisdom, was applying Strategy II—sending them to the right place at the right time. All night

116

long they had been in the wrong place at the wrong time.

As always, it paid to obey Jesus. They got such a great catch of fish that they filled one of their boats and had to call for the other. If a third boat had been available, that one probably would have been filled as well. The new program was producing results, and the fishermen were delighted.

So was Jesus. His disciples had learned a valuable lesson. They trusted their Lord, and He was able to put them in the right place at the right time.

That phrase, *"launch out into the deep,"* rings down to us today. It is another of the great missionary commands of the Bible.

Thousands of Christians in North America would like to be more deeply involved in missions. They want to "launch out into the deep," but they don't quite know how. They feel that Jesus has something more for them to do in missions, and they would like to discover what it is. They want to know the right place and the right time.

This whole book has been written precisely to help you find God's specific time and place for you. If you have read the book, you have taken a significant first step. Now here are some concrete hints as to how to go to the mission field, how to use your money for missions, how to learn more about missions, and how to get a mission program going in your church.

How to Go to the Mission Field

There are four ways to go to the mission field:

1. You can go as a career missionary. If you want to investigate the possibilities of becoming a career missionary, the first thing to do is to talk to your pastor. Chances are he will give you some denominational contacts, and he may know of some interdenominational boards as well.

I suggest that you write to the two large evangelical

associations of missions and ask them for   a) a listing of their affiliated mission boards, and   b) a list of current openings, if available. The members of these associations have to meet certain standards which other boards might not meet, so they are dependable. Then write for more detail to the specific boards that seem to interest you. Here are the addresses:

Interdenominational Foreign Mission Association
P.O. Box 395
Wheaton, IL 60187

Evangelical Foreign Missions Association
1405 G Street, N.W.
Washington, D.C. 20005

If at all possible, try to attend a large missionary conference where several mission boards will send representatives. The granddaddy of them all is the Inter-Varsity Christian Fellowship conference, held on the Urbana campus of the University of Illinois during the Christmas holidays every three years. Almost every mission board is represented there by its best people. Most of them print new, up-to-date literature on their work specially for that conference, because they are very much interested in recruiting new workers there. For further information write:

Inter-Varsity Christian Fellowship
233 Langdon Street
Madison, WI 53703

Choose a mission board with care. Be sure to ask enough questions so you are assured that you are joining a team you will enjoy living and working with, and the team is one in which you will be encouraged to use your own spiritual gifts, as far as you can identify them now. Other things being equal, the place where you will be working is secondary. The most important thing is joining the right team.

That's why, when you narrow down the field, you should thoroughly investigate more than one board, possibly two or three. Only by making intelligent comparisons will you be reasonably sure you are not making a mistake.

2. *You can go as a short-term worker.* Short-term service is especially appropriate for Christian people who have a skill, who want to donate a portion of their lives to making a significant contribution to God's work on the foreign field, and who are not confined to home. Those who have children at home generally should not consider short-term service. But single people, younger couples, and older couples can all find opportunities for short-term service.

Unless you already know of opportunities, you will find two organizations helpful as a starter. The first is Short Terms Abroad, which publishes a free 74-page booklet called *Opportunities,* and updates it by computer every year. It is the most complete listing available of openings for short-term missionary service. Address:

Short Terms Abroad
Box 575
Downers Grove, IL 60515

This booklet also contains a "personal profile" form which will match your qualifications with opportunities through a computer at the headquarters of Intercristo. This personalized service will cost you five dollars. If interested, you may also write directly to:

Intercristo
Box 9323
Seattle, WA 98109

The second contact to make is the Christian Service Corps. They are, as their name suggests, a Christian parallel to the Peace Corps. They do not just match you up with missions as Short Terms Abroad and Intercristo do. They send you out to work with existing missions, but you go as their own CSC "corpsman" and with their training. If interested, write for their *Question and Answer Booklet* to:

Christian Service Corps
1509 Sixteenth Street, N.W.
Washington, D.C. 20036

3. You can go as a summer student. The best contacts for summer students are your church, your school, or your denominational mission board. Denominations like Assemblies of God, Church of the Nazarene, Christian and Missionary Alliance, and scores of others have programs that your pastor can put you in touch with. If you run into a dead end there, here are two places that will help you:

Spearhead Program
285 Orchard Terrace
Bogota, NJ 07603

Operation Mobilization
Box 148
Midland Park, NJ 07432

4. You can go as a visitor. In order to do this, you will need to have a personal contact on the mission field of your choice. Consult with your friend or relative first, then make arrangements with a travel agent. Travel agents are paid by the airlines and do not charge clients. If you prefer a specially arranged tour, you can get information from:

Gotaas World Travel
7 West Madison Street
Chicago, IL

Universal Travel Service, Inc.
Countryside Mall Box 874
Palatine, IL 60067

Menno Travel Service
800 Second Avenue
New York, NY 10017

How to Use Your Money for Missions

As you might have suspected, there are some shysters trying to siphon off some of the $350 million which go to missions each year. Happily, there aren't too many, and the word soon gets around when one turns up. But don't be careless in your giving.

A good bit of money goes to missions through local church missionary programs. A church missionary committee that is aware of the matters explained in chapters 4 and 5 knows how to handle missionary funds responsibly.

There are good reasons, however, why some Christians prefer to give at least some of their contributions directly to mission boards. In any case, be sure that (1) it is a reputable organization (membership in IFMA or EFMA or a similar organization assures this); and that (2) your gifts are tax-deductible. You can get a free pamphlet entitled "Giving to Missions: How to Make it Tax-Deductible" from:

Evangelical Missions Information Service
Box 794
Wheaton, IL 60187

Many Christians are unaware of substantial opportunities for good financial stewardship for the cause of missions apart from direct giving. Several mission boards have well-developed stewardship departments that offer free financial advice to interested persons. They will help you make out your will properly so that your estate will do what you want it to do rather than what the government wants it to; they will steer you into wise investments, which not only may earn you more returns now, but which will help missionary work as well; they will explain tax advantages you otherwise may not know about; and they will help you avoid costly financial mistakes.

If you are not in contact with a Christian organization that can help you in these somewhat complex financial matters, you may write and ask for free information from either of two organizations which have accumulated a great deal of experience in Christian stewardship:

Fuller Evangelistic Association
Box 989
Pasadena, CA 91102

World Vision International
919 West Huntington Drive
Monrovia, CA 91016

How to Learn More About Missions

If you have digested the preceding eight chapters, you are probably excited about missions. But your appetite, hopefully, has also been whetted for more. The next eighteen books have already been listed under the section "for further reading" at the end of each chapter. For specific guidance, see the Self-Study Missionary Reading List immediately following this chapter.

In order to keep up on the latest and best in missionary publishing, however, you will want to join the Church Growth Book Club. This costs only one dollar per year, and the membership will also bring you, every two months, the *Church Growth Bulletin,* one of the nation's outstanding missionary periodicals. Membership in the Church Growth Book Club does not commit you to buy any minimum number of books during the year. It does offer you substantial savings on almost all missionary literature. Write:

Church Growth Book Club
533 Hermosa Street
South Pasadena, CA 91030

The best of scholarly-level evangelical reading on missions is found in *Evangelical Missions Quarterly,* a joint publication of EFMA and IFMA. It costs $4.25 per year and is available from:

Evangelical Missions Quarterly
Box 267
Springfield, Pennsylvania 19064

There is no popular Christian magazine exclusively devoted to missions, although such favorites as *Moody Monthly, Christian Life, Christianity Today,* and *Eternity* publish good missionary articles from time to time. Each mission board has its own publication, which they will send you if you contribute to the organization, or in many cases if you simply request it. *World Vision* magazine is one of the most informative of these. Here are the addresses:

Moody Monthly
820 N. La Salle Street
Chicago, IL 60610

Christian Life
Gundersen Drive and Schmale Road
Wheaton, IL 60187

Christianity Today
Washington Building
Washington, D.C. 20005

Eternity
1716 Spruce Street
Philadelphia, PA 19103

World Vision
919 W. Huntington Drive
Monrovia, CA 91016

Although it is rather expensive (twenty-five dollars per year), becoming an "associate" of Evangelical Missions Information Service will bring you the frontline, executive-level publications in the field of evangelical missions. As an EMIS Associate you receive twenty-four issues per year of *Missionary News Service,* regular mailings of *Pulse* area editions for Latin America, Africa, Asia, Europe, and the Muslim World, four issues per year of *Evangelical Missions Quarterly,* the top scholarly evangelical missions journal, and the *EMIS Bulletin.* The address:

Evangelical Missions Information Service
Box 794
Wheaton, IL 60187

As your interest in missions grows, you may want to take some systematic studies. You can do this on three levels:

1. Correspondence courses. The Moody Bible Institute has some excellent correspondence courses in missions, on both Bible institute and college level. Write:

Moody Bible Institute Correspondence School
820 North La Salle Street
Chicago, IL 60610

2. Seminars and workshops. The Evangelical Foreign Missions Association sponsors a series of seminars on church growth for foreign missionary candidates each year in different parts of the country. You can get a listing of the dates and places by writing: 1405 G. Street, N.W., Washington, D.C. 20005.

3. Formal studies. If you live in the vicinity of a Bible institute or theological seminary, inquire about courses in missions they make available to laymen. If you can afford two weeks of time during the summer, Wheaton College conducts a Summer Institute of Missions, offering a variety of electives that carry full college credit. Write:

Wheaton College
Summer Institute of Missions
Wheaton, IL 60187

How to Get a Missions Program Going in Your Church

The starting ingredients for a local church missionary program are a pastor who is excited about missions and who will give his support to the program, a missionary chairman who will make missions his or her avocation, and a dedicated missionary committee.

As the groundwork is laid, all committee members should study this book and other missionary literature. Your denomination probably has some literature on how to start missionary programs, and perhaps denominational advisors are available. Your pastor will know.

Overseas Crusades has a program to assist local churches. They publish a bulletin called *Church Missionary Helps Quarterly,* an 8-page resource and idea interchange with news of local church mission programs. For a year's subscription send $2.00 to:

Missionary Helps
Box 66
Palo Alto, California 94302

Here are five specific suggestions:

1. Organize a missionary conference. If it has never been done, the missionary committee chairman needs to get some experience in this by visiting other conferences, talking to leaders of churches that have successful conferences, consulting with mission board representatives, and reading what he can find. The literature on this is not vast, but here are some books and where you can get them:

Building Blocks for the Missionary Program of the Church and Missionary Idea Kit
Conservative Baptist Missionary Societies
Box 5
Wheaton, IL 60187

Missionary Education Helps for the Local Church
By Dick Pearson
Overseas Crusades
265 Lytton Avenue
Palo Alto, CA 94301

A Successful Missionary Program in Your Church
By Willis E. Garrett
Back to the Bible Broadcast
12th and M Streets
Lincoln, NB 68500

Promoting Missions in the Local Church
By Kerry Lovering
Sudan Interior Mission
Cedar Grove, NJ 07009

The purpose of the missionary conference is to inform, inspire, and challenge. Many of the larger IFMA/EFMA mission boards are happy to offer free consultation service for churches that want to set up a missionary conference.

Missions are glad to do this because, as we said in chapter 4, missions need churches as legs need the body. Mutually helpful contact with local churches is the lifeblood of mission agencies.

2. *Take on the personal support of one or more missionaries.* Some guidelines for missionary support are laid down in chapter 5. Try to get a large slice of the support of at least one missionary so the church will develop the feeling that he is "our missionary in Mamba Bamba." Missionary societies, your own denomination, or contacts your church members already have will soon uncover possibilities for supporting workers compatible with your church people.

3. *Bring in missionary speakers between conferences.* Missions should not be just a once-a-year shot for the church. If the church is to become a missionary church, missions must appear in the church program all year long. Missionary speakers are not expensive. Very few have a fixed honorarium, but the church should be careful not to take advantage of this. Calculate reasonable mileage expenses for his travel, and add an honorarium of twenty to seventy-five dollars on top of it. These costs can be built into the missionary committee's budget.

4. *Keep good literature flowing through the church.* One of the best devices for keeping a congregation up on what is happening in missions is the monthly church bulletin insert published by Tyndale House (of *The Living Bible* fame). The inserts cost only $1.50 per month per hundred. If interested, write:

The Church Around the World
Tyndale House Publishers
336 Gundersen Drive
Wheaton, IL 60187

Some Christian periodicals offer special bulk subscriptions to churches. One that gives substantial space to missionary information of all kinds is *Today's Christian,* published by the radio broadcast, "The Joyful Sound." This 12-page paper costs twelve cents each up to one hundred and ten cents each over one hundred and is available from:

The Joyful Sound
Box 123
Los Angeles, CA 90053

5. Send some young people to the mission field.
Summer student programs are becoming increasingly helpful in getting local churches directly involved in missions through young people. Such programs are described in several other places in this book, but here I would like to suggest more local church involvement. Summer students need support. It is always good to let them have the experience of raising some of their own support, but the local church should be behind them as well.

Get on Board

God is pleased when his people exercise their faith and "launch out into the deep." He wants you to launch out with your mind, with your talents, and with your money. If you have read this book, you have received the challenge.
The rest is up to you.

For further reading:
Griffiths, Michael C. *Give Up Your Small Ambitions; What You've Always Wanted to Know About Becoming a Missionary.* Chicago: Moody Press, 1971.
Neill, Stephen. *Call to Mission.* Philadelphia: Fortress Press, 1970.

A Self-Study
Missionary Reading List

The following is a priority reading list including many of the books mentioned at the ends of chapters. By *priority* I mean that the books here are listed in the order you should read them, at least in my opinion. Almost every book on the list is available from the Church Growth Book Club (see page 125).

A Manual for Evangelism/Church Growth by Vergil Gerber (South Pasadena, William Carey Library, 1973), paper.

Understanding Church Growth by Donald McGavran (Grand Rapids, Eerdmans, 1970), cloth and paper.

Church Growth and the Word of God by Alan R. Tippett (Grand Rapids, Eerdmans, 1970), paper.

Frontiers in Missionary Strategy by C. Peter Wagner (Chicago, Moody Press, 1971), cloth.

The Twenty-five Unbelievable Years, 1945-1969, by Ralph D. Winter (South Pasadena, William Carey Library, 1969), paper.

Give Up Your Small Ambitions by Michael C. Griffiths (Chicago, Moody Press, 1971), paper.

Look Out! The Pentecostals Are Coming by C. Peter Wagner (Carol Stream, Creation House, 1973), cloth.

Call to Mission by Stephen Neill (Philadelphia, Fortress Press, 1970), cloth.

Crucial Issues in Missions Tomorrow, edited by Donald McGavran (Chicago, Moody Press, 1972), cloth.

The Warp and the Woof by Ralph D. Winter and R.

Pierce Beaver (South Pasadena, William Carey Library, 1970), paper.

Church/Mission Tensions Today, edited by C. Peter Wagner (Chicago, Moody Press, 1972), cloth.

A Global View of Christian Missions by J. Herbert Kane (Grand Rapids, Baker Book House, 1971), cloth.

Missions from the Third World by James Wong, Peter Larson, and Edward Pentecost (Singapore, Church Growth Study Center, 1973), paper.

Winds of Change in Christian Mission by J. Herbert Kane (Chicago, Moody Press, 1973), paper.

God, Man and Church Growth, edited by Alan R. Tippett (Grand Rapids, Eerdmans, 1973), cloth.

The Validity of the Christian Mission by Elton Trueblood, (New York, Harper & Row, 1972), cloth.

Forward Through the Ages by Basil Mathews (New York, Friendship Press, 1960), cloth.

An Extension Seminary Primer by Ralph R. Covell and C. Peter Wagner (South Pasadena, William Carey Library, 1971), paper.

Response: The Church in Mission to a World in Crisis by James A. Cogswell (Richmond, CLC Press, 1971), paper.

A Biblical Theology of Missions by George W. Peters (Chicago, Moody Press, 1972), cloth.

Missions: Which Way? and *Shaken Foundations* by Peter Beyerhaus (Grand Rapids, Zondervan Publishing House, 1971 and 1972), both in paper.

Manual for Accepted Missionary Candidates by Marjorie A. Collins (South Pasadena, William Carey Library, 1972), paper.

Eye of the Storm, edited by Donald McGavran (Waco, Word Books, 1972), cloth.

An Evangelical Theology of Missions by Harold Lindsell (Grand Rapids, Zondervan Publishing House, 1970), paper.

The Inescapable Calling by R. Kenneth Strachan (Grand Rapids, Eerdmans, 1968), paper.

Index

131